TAKE
BACK
YOUR
TIME

Delight yourself in the LORD and he will
give you the desires of your heart.
—Psalm 37:4 ESV

TAKE
BACK
YOUR
TIME

The Guilt-Free
Guide to Life
Balance

CHRISTY WRIGHT

RAMSEY
PRESS

Published by Ramsey Press, The Lampo Group, LLC
Franklin, Tennessee 37064

Editors: Jennifer Gingerich and Rachel Knapp
Cover Design: Chris Carrico and Gretchen Hyer
Interior Design: PerfecType, Nashville, TN

ISBN: 9781942121565

Library of Congress Cataloging-in-Publication Data
Names: Wright, Christy, author.
Title: Take back your time : the guilt-free guide to life balance / Christy Wright.
Description: Franklin, Tennessee : Ramsey Press, [2021] | Includes bibliographical references.
Identifiers: LCCN 2021014607 | ISBN 9781942121565 (hardcover) | ISBN 9781942121572 (ebook)
Subjects: LCSH: Time management. | Time management--Religious aspects--Christianity. | Work-life balance.
Classification: LCC BF637.T5 W75 2021 | DDC 640/.43--dc23
LC record available at https://lccn.loc.gov/2021014607

Printed in the United States of America
21 22 23 24 25 WRZ 5 4 3 2 1

For my amazing husband, Matt.

Matt, you are patient. You are kind. You
don't envy others and you don't boast. You
aren't proud and you aren't rude. You aren't
self-seeking. You aren't easily angered and
you don't keep a record of wrongs.
You are truly the definition of love.
This book is about how to create balance in a life
you love and are proud of, and the only reason
I've been able to do that is because of you.
I love our family, I love our life, and most of all,
I love you.

CONTENTS

Acknowledgments ix

Foreword xiii

Introduction 1

Chapter 1 Redefining Balance 9

Chapter 2 The Path to Balance 35

Chapter 3 Step 1: Decide What Matters 53

Chapter 4 Step 2: Stop Doing What Doesn't Matter 85

Chapter 5 Step 3: Create a Schedule That Reflects What Matters 105

Chapter 6 Step 4: Protect What Matters 133

Chapter 7 Step 5: Be Present for What Matters 165

Chapter 8 Creating Balance in Every Season 189

Conclusion 211

Notes 219

ACKNOWLEDGMENTS

I can't believe I get to do this. I would have never in a million years dreamed that I would get to write my own book one day, much less multiple books. Each book represents not only a new dream but an incredible team who has worked tirelessly to bring that dream and that book to life.

There are several people in particular I want to say a special thank-you to.

First, to my editor Jen Gingerich: Jen, I am so thankful for the many ways you have taught me and led me and shaped me into a stronger writer through this process. This book is so much better because of you, and I'm grateful for all of your hard work that got us here. You helped me shake off my own guilt in the writing process in ways you don't even realize.

Rachel Knapp, Amy McCollom, Caitlin Cofield, Jasmine Cannady, Eva Daniel, Jennifer Day, and the entire Ramsey Press team, thank you for the heart and hard work you poured into this. You owned this book and contributed ideas and suggestions that made it so much more impactful.

ACKNOWLEDGMENTS

Chris Carrico, Gretchen Hyer, and Seth Farmer, I am so grateful for how encouraging you were through the whole cover design process. You let me bring crazy ideas to the table and even helped make them happen.

Elizabeth Cole, thank you for helping to get this message out into the world. You work harder than anyone even realizes, and I'm so grateful for all you do for me and this team.

Kristyna Murphy, you do *everything* for *everything*. I don't know how you thank someone for that, but thank you. Your fingerprint is on every single thing we do, and I couldn't do it without you.

Preston Cannon, thank you for leading this entire initiative. You and I have worked together for so long, and I am always grateful for your friendship and leadership through each project. I love to write and am thankful you help make it happen.

Jeremy Breland, Suzanne Simms, Luke LeFevre, Jen Sievertsen, and the entire leadership team, thank you for all of the many ways you have poured into me over the years and continue to. I am better because of each of you.

Dave Ramsey, for giving me the job of a lifetime. I'm thankful every day that you took a chance on me, and I still can't believe I get to do this.

Tyler Seymour, my brand manager, and Bekah Stallard, our nanny, you are two people who have literally changed my life. Tyler, you've changed my work life. You've helped me work smarter, be kinder, and overall be better in every aspect of my job. I have no idea how I did anything before you joined the team. Bekah, you have changed my home life. You love our children like they are your own and you have made this book—and every project I work on—possible because of all you do and all you are to our family. Having any sense of balance in my life has only been possible because of both of you.

To my mom, my dad and stepmom Diane, and my mother- and father-in-law, Pam and Forrest, thank you for all the ways you love and help me—whether that's watching the kids or helping with one of our unending house projects. Each of you love and support our family so well. You are the greatest grandparents our children could ever have and I'm thankful for the many ways you've encouraged me personally through this journey.

Carter, Conley, and Mary Grace, of all the things I've ever accomplished in my entire life, nothing even comes close to the joy I get to experience being your mom. I love each of you more than you can possibly imagine, and I'm so proud of you.

Matt, if there is anyone in the world who could balance me out, it's you. You are everything I am not, and you challenge me to be better in a million different ways. You are at the center of everything that matters to me, and I'm so grateful for all of your sacrifice and support that made this book possible. I love this life we've created, and most of all, I love you.

To you, my reader, thank you for picking up this book. I've heard your stories, your fears, and your frustrations around this topic of balance for over a decade. So many of you contributed to this book in ways you don't even realize, and my passion for this topic comes from getting to walk this out with you for so long. Because of you, I couldn't *not* write this book. Thank you for helping me inject hope into a topic that desperately needs it. This book came to life because of, and for, *you*.

FOREWORD
BY DAVE RAMSEY

I tried to talk her out of it. I pictured her on that daunting stage in front of a bunch of hungry sharks, and I was convinced she'd get eaten alive.

It was a stage I'd been on many times before. I knew the audience would be made of hundreds of business leaders from all across the country. But not just any business leaders. These were high-octane business owners and entrepreneurs who get things done. These were women and men who were singularly focused on getting their businesses up and running. They were worried about building profit margins, optimal marketing strategies, and peak-performing teams. I was certain they would not be impressed by the soft topic that Christy Wright, our newest Ramsey Personality, was proposing to speak to them about. As a matter of fact, I thought they might be offended by it.

But there we sat, hashing out the idea of Christy doing her first EntreLeadership Master Series (EMS) talk on *life balance*. If you heard the sing-song sarcasm entwined in the italics just now, you heard right. That's where my mind was at the time. This was our company's tactical five-day business event where you learn the entire Ramsey playbook for how to successfully run and grow your business, and draws a no-nonsense crowd. I was convinced *life balance* wasn't tough enough for such a tough audience. But Christy was passionate about the subject and just wouldn't relent. So I agreed to put her on the stage . . . and let her learn her lesson.

Even with all my forewarning, Christy confidently took the stage at EMS that year in front of that sea of sharks. And once again, I discovered that some of my biggest hits happen when I'm wrong. She was a hit! The topic was a hit! The people absolutely came unglued. Christy had touched a nerve, and it was a total cryfest. She had been right all along.

The reason I pushed back against the subject of *life balance* was not just because it seemed soft for that particular audience. It's because I think it's a topic that's become universally toxic and full of shame. It's out of control. And it's a freaking illusion! At least the way culture tells it.

Of course, we all instinctually recognize that we need to spend our time on things that will make us smile at the end of our life. Who doesn't want a life full of fulfilling moments? But that's certainly not achieved by perfectly touching all the bases of your life all in one perfectly balanced little day and then cryogenically freezing a template of that perfectly balanced little day to live on repeat over and over again. That's just ridiculous—and unachievable.

People who are successful in marriage, or who raise successful kids, or who run successful businesses, are actually *out* of balance. That's why I don't like the unrealistic way our culture has defined *life balance*. Again, it's the ultimate illusion. People are loaded up with a bunch of guilt about things they *should* be doing, but they're always thinking about the wrong things. I believe that's why the hardcore EMS audience responded in such an emotional way to Christy's message. She called out the shoulds, the guilt, the fixation on all the wrong things, and she gave everyone a refreshing take on *real* life balance. It was a countercultural message they desperately needed to hear then, and it's a message just as important for us now.

The great news is, Christy's passion for the topic of *real* life balance has only grown. She's continued to study, research, and speak on this subject. She's analyzed her own experiences and heard countless stories from real-life people about their real-life struggles. She's dug deep into Scripture to learn what God says about having balance, peace, and purpose in our lives. And all of this has led her to find a clear path to help us get what we want out of this life without internalizing the toxic, misguided *life balance* messages that exist in our culture today.

As you read, it's going to make perfect sense to you. And I suspect that you, like that EMS audience of long ago, will have a smile on your face and maybe your eyes will even leak. You might cry tears of relief, realizing you no longer have to beat yourself up for all the balls you can't seem to keep in the air at one time. You might experience breakthrough, recognizing and reclaiming all that you've lost by being focused on the wrong things for way too long. Either way, I can promise you that your life will be changed if you apply these practical principles. Christy will show you what *real* life balance looks like. And she'll give you the tools you need to help you focus on the right things, right now, to build a life that truly reflects what matters most to you.

INTRODUCTION

I was exhausted.

It was May of 2016, and day after day, week after week, I had this feeling of tightness in my chest. I was five months pregnant with my second son, Conley, working on my first book, launching a podcast, and traveling to speak. I would wake up early, stay up late, and run as hard and as fast as I could every minute in between, desperately trying to keep up. But no matter how hard or smart I worked, or how many tasks I checked off my to-do list each day, it wasn't enough. I felt like I was trying to climb out of quicksand.

One day I decided to sit down and type it all out, and I mean *all* of it—every last project due, every meeting I'd committed to, and every responsibility I had for the month. I added up the hours needed to get everything done. It totaled 440 hours. Then I looked at my schedule to see how many hours I had to work with. If I used every available minute of each day, I had 423 hours. So even if I worked every waking minute, if I never ate or took a bathroom break, I *still* wouldn't get it all done. It was in that moment I realized something had to change.

You may be wondering how I got myself into that situation. Did I have unrealistic expectations for how long things would take? Probably. Did I overcommit myself? Definitely. Did I struggle with saying no and prioritizing? For sure. But this wasn't the first time I was overwhelmed, overcommitted, and out of balance. I'd been there many times before. And the fact that you're reading this book right now tells me you've probably been there too.

LIFE BALANCE IS A MOVING TARGET

No matter where I'm speaking across the country, the question I'm asked most often is, How do you balance it all? It's the million-dollar question, isn't it? We all want to know the answer.

How do you keep up with the pace of life, manage your time, and make decisions?

How do you shake the shadow of guilt that seems to follow you wherever you go?

How do you do all the right things—and how do you even know what the right things are?

INTRODUCTION

When you think of "life balance," certain images might come to mind: spinning plates, juggling balls, walking a tight-rope. Why? Because many of us have this idea that in order to be balanced, we have to do everything equally. And we have to do it all the time and do it all well. We have mile-long to-do lists and think if we could just get it all done—if we could just be productive enough, efficient enough, *good* enough—then finally, *finally* we will feel balanced. So we work harder, stay up later, and juggle faster.

But it never works, does it?

We feel like we have to do it all, and then feel guilty when we can't. We want to find balance—whatever that means for each of us—but it's like chasing a moving target. How in the world are we supposed to achieve balance if we can't define it or pin it down? Most of us don't even know what balance is, but we're all acutely aware that we don't have it. And then we always think we know just how to solve our balance problem: *I just need more time! I just need more hours in a day!* We can't find more time of course, so we just end up discouraged.

No matter what we do or how hard we try, we always seem to end up at the same place: feeling exhausted and like we're failing.

YOU'RE DOING A GOOD JOB

After having our first son, Carter, I hit a low point. From the terrifying emergency cesarean section, to a trip back to the emergency room two days after being discharged, to fighting infections and the complete nightmare that nursing turned out to be for us—it was all a really difficult blur.

But there was one night I remember vividly. It was three o'clock in the morning, and I was in the nursery rocking my screaming son in the glider. When my husband, Matt, heard crying on the monitor and realized it was not one but two voices crying out, he jumped up to see what was wrong. He ran into the nursery and found me sobbing along with my son, crying a deep and desperate cry of defeat with the last bit of energy I had. When Matt could see no one was hurt but that I was at the end of everything I had, he stood in the doorway, looked at me, and with both a sweetness and sternness in his voice, he said just five words:

"You're doing a good job."

I cried harder because I wanted so badly for that to be true. He said those words again and again—with the same certainty every time.

"You're *doing* a good job."

"You're doing a *good* job."

Like many new parents, I felt like I was failing. Like I couldn't do anything right. Like I wasn't enough. While those feelings were very real for me at the time, they weren't true.

That's why what my husband said to me was so powerful. It wasn't a surface-level compliment. It was a statement of truth that cut through the lie that had been weighing me down.

Whether you're adjusting to becoming a parent for the first time or you've had a hard season at work or you're just dealing with the overwhelm of the day-to-day grind, many people carry around the heavy and exhausting belief that they aren't enough. Have you ever felt like that? Maybe you feel like that right now. Like you aren't doing enough, you aren't efficient enough, you aren't making enough money, you aren't keeping your house clean enough, your kids aren't well-behaved enough. *You* aren't enough. And the feeling that you're failing haunts you at every corner.

But you're not failing.

You're not.

You are doing a good job.

You're doing so many things right. And you are already enough for this life you're leading.

I'm going to help you create your version of balance where you can let your shoulders relax, get the right things done, have some fun, and actually enjoy your life. But before we do, I want you to begin this journey with a very important truth. You're *already* doing a good job.

BREAKING FREE

You shouldn't be haunted by this elusive idea of balancing it all, wondering why you can't seem to achieve balance while the apparent lack of it steals your joy, your rest, your relationships, and your very sense of self. You weren't created to live busy and burnt out, unhappy and unfulfilled. There's more for you in this life. There's more for you to experience and appreciate and enjoy, and not just when you get through your to-do list. There's more for you right now. Today.

Being a mom of three young kids with a busy career and a lot of interests, I know what it's like to be stretched too thin. And after years of trying and failing, of overcommitting then becoming frustrated and resentful, I realized I had more control over my lack of balance than I wanted to believe. And it wasn't just a matter of saying no to a few things in order to release the pressure valve on my life. I had to get a handle on *why* I kept getting myself into these predicaments to begin with.

Here's what I have discovered: Balance doesn't come from getting more done. You don't need more hours in a day and I don't either. *More* time isn't the answer because balance isn't a math problem.

Balance isn't as much about something you *do*, how you *"balance it all."* Balance—real balance that we all crave—is something else entirely. It's something you create and feel and become in your life. It is being confident in who you are, the choices you're making, and the life you're creating. It feels like peace even when you're surrounded by chaos. It's finally shaking the guilt that's been nagging at you for so long and giving yourself permission to be proud of what you're doing. It feels like a long, deep breath after years of shallow breathing. Like stepping off the treadmill after running yourself ragged for so long. It feels like freedom—freedom to be the person you want to be and to create the life you want to lead. Whether we realize it or not, that's the type of balance we really want and that's the type of balance we are going to talk about creating in the pages ahead.

In *Take Back Your Time*, we're going to dig deep and get to the root of what's going on. We're not going to just scratch the surface by looking at the latest and greatest time-management apps or talking about how to do more in less time. This is not a productivity book. Balance is less about finding hours to add to your day and more about finding peace, fulfillment, and confidence in how you use the hours you already have.

And I don't want you to just read about life balance either. I want you to actually create it in your life. That's why at the end of each chapter, you will see journal questions for you to think about and a challenge with practical steps for you to complete. I've even created a free digital workbook that follows along with this book to help you put everything you're learning into practice. You can download that at ramseysolutions .com/tbyt. The workbook follows along with this book chapter by chapter. It has worksheets for you to use to complete the challenge for each chapter, and it has templates and exercises so you can customize your entire experience on this journey. Download your Take Back Your Time Workbook before you dive into chapter 1 so you can keep up with your notes and plans for creating balance every step of the way.

We know we have a problem when it comes to achieving balance—the good news is, there's a solution. I'm going to show you how you can break free from the never-ending busyness and crazy pace of life. I'm going to help you create balance so you can let your shoulders relax, get the right things done, have some fun, and actually *enjoy* your life.

Are you ready? Let's do this!

CHAPTER 1

REDEFINING BALANCE

When my first child, Carter, was about a year old, he cried nonstop for two weeks. He was cutting teeth around that time and the pain was excruciating for him. We tried all the tricks for teething—giving him teething toys, freezing wet washcloths for him to chew on, rubbing baby Orajel on his little gums to try to relieve his discomfort—but nothing worked. He was inconsolable.

Finally, when my husband, Matt, and I had exhausted our list of ideas, I took Carter to the pediatrician. As Carter sat in my lap, the doctor took one look in his ears and said matter-of-factly, "He has an ear infection." Oh . . . Right. Our poor little guy probably wondered what in the world we were doing rubbing his gums with numbing ointment and shoving frozen washcloths in his mouth when it was his ears, not his teeth, giving him so much pain.

But you know what? When you don't know what the problem is, you can't fix it. We've all experienced a situation like this at some point, haven't we? We try desperately to fix a problem that we think we know the answer to, when in reality we don't even know what the problem is to begin with. And the same is true with our ideas about life balance.

HOW DID WE GET HERE?

Before we try to understand our problem with life balance, let's look at a few root causes by asking the question: *How did we even get here?* How did we get to this place of overwhelmed and unfulfilled, busy and burnt out? How did we end up feeling like victims to our schedules and prisoners of our to-do lists? When did we stop having fun and, even worse, stop *being* fun?

Part of the problem is that our world is out of balance. But similar to your life and mine, that didn't happen overnight. Over the past thirty, forty, fifty years, the world has gradually gained speed. From personal computers entering the picture in the 1970s to the global internet in the 1980s to the earliest smartphones being introduced in the mid 1990s, our world has become more advanced, more efficient, and a whole lot faster.

Then social media invaded our lives. In 2004, Facebook launched. In 2005, YouTube was created, and in 2006, Twitter was introduced. Then in 2007, the iPhone allowed us to carry tiny computers in our pockets with our email, our calendars, and all the information we could ever need, including a lot that we don't need. We are now "on call" all day, every day. That's exhausting.

And while the amount of information available to you, the demands on your time, and the expectations you feel are infinite, your time is excruciatingly finite. You still only have twenty-four hours in a day to get it all done.

But the breakneck speed of our culture and nonstop nature of technology aren't completely to blame. We add our own set of issues to the problem as well. We have trouble saying no, we struggle to set boundaries, we have an unhealthy need to be needed, we love pleasing people, and we can't prioritize for the life of us! We want to be all things to all people all the time, and all we end up feeling is tired and guilty because there's too much to do and we can't do it all. No wonder we feel out of balance!

A NEW DEFINITION OF LIFE BALANCE

When we talk about life balance, we're usually referring to how we divide our time between our work life and our home life.

Maybe you've always thought life balance means working 50 percent of the time and having a life 50 percent of the time. Or maybe you think it means doing everything for an equal amount of time, like dividing a pie into perfectly equal parts or spinning all those plates.

When something feels off with that balance, we often try to fix our calendars and our to-do lists. We think, *I just need to be more efficient and more productive.* We tweak and shift things around, thinking we can come up with some magic solution that will help us feel perfectly balanced. But even after all of our fixing, we still feel as if something's not quite right.

That's because balance doesn't come from getting more done. You and I have tried that, and it hasn't worked. Here's the good news: there's a way to create balance that *does* work.

I'm going to give you a new definition of life balance that will not only guide how you manage your time but will also empower you to shake the guilt that's been nagging at you and empower you to actually be present for whatever is in front of you. This is the finish line we're going to work toward through the rest of this book. Are you ready for it? Here it is:

Life balance isn't about doing everything for an equal amount of time. Life balance is about doing the right things at the right time. It's about spending your one life on what matters to you.

By that definition, you actually *can* achieve balance! Balance isn't about productivity or efficiency or your to-do list. It's not about getting *more* time or *more* done. It's about getting rid of the exhaustion and guilt so you can find peace and fulfillment in your one life. And believe it or not, it's possible!

But if we think life balance is about equally dividing our time, we set ourselves up to fail. We make it impossible to adapt to the season we're in. Having a perfect split between how you spend your time isn't just unrealistic—it's not even desirable. If you try to shape your day so that you can schedule everything for an equal amount of time, you'll never create momentum and never be able to chase big goals or grow in any area of your life. And you'll never have margin for anything new.

> Having a perfect split between how you spend your time isn't just unrealistic—it's not even desirable.

Imagine an Olympic triathlete who trains for thirty hours a week to prepare for a big race. All of his energy is focused on training, getting enough sleep, and making sure his mind and body are ready to compete. Is he out of balance?

What about the new mom whose entire days are consumed with feeding, changing, and nurturing her newborn baby and has zero time for a social life? Is she out of balance? How about the business owner who's working seven days a week to get his business off the ground or the law-school graduate working seventy hours a week trying to build her career? Are these people out of balance because they don't have some mystical equilibrium between their *work* and their *life*?

The athlete training for thirty-plus hours a week and the new mom pouring all her time into her child are doing what matters most to them in this season of their lives. Same with that business owner trying to get his business off the ground and the young lawyer trying to build her career—they're doing the right thing at the right time and focusing on what matters most to them. From the outside, they may not look balanced at all because they're not dividing their time evenly. But as they spend their time on what matters most to them, regardless of how that may look to someone else, they will feel a sense of balance and find their own version of balance.

And that's exactly what I want to help you do too. We're going to talk about how to figure out what's important to you in any season of life you might be in, and then how to spend your time on those things to create your version of balance. But first, let's take a deep dive into why we feel out of balance in the first place. This will help us solve our balance problem at the root level, and it will help us make different and better decisions moving forward.

WHY WE FEEL OUT OF BALANCE

When we feel out of balance, we first need to understand *why* we feel this way. I've found there are four main reasons: (1) We're doing *too many* things. (2) We're *not doing enough* things. (3) We're doing the *wrong* things. (4) We're not doing the *right* things. Let's look at each of these.

Reason #1: We're doing too many things.

It's no surprise to anyone that the pace of life just keeps moving faster. We have more demands on us than ever before, and our solution isn't to cut things out or slow down. It's to multitask and run faster to keep up. We want to be *more* efficient and *more* productive so we can do *more*.

Instead of saying no, we try to wedge one more thing in. We have no margin in our time, and we run ourselves into the ground trying to get it all done. We treat our calendar like I treat my suitcase when I travel. I cram it as full as possible, and when it doesn't all fit, I open the extender zipper and shove things into the top pockets. By the time I'm done packing, I couldn't slide a bobby pin in it if I wanted to. My suitcase is bulging at every seam, and even though it's carry-on size, there's no way it would fit in the overhead compartment with how much I've crammed in. It's exhausting to carry and hard to maneuver. It also doesn't leave any room for anything new that I might want to get while on my trip.

We do this with our schedules too. We pretend we're the Energizer Bunny that can just keep going and going and going, but we aren't—and we can't. As long as we cram more into our schedules than they can comfortably hold, we will never feel balanced and we'll never have room for anything new. Doing too many things always leaves us feeling stressed, rushed, exhausted, and anxious.

Reason #2: We're not doing enough things.

The opposite problem of doing too many things is not doing enough things. Many of us experienced this in a very real way when COVID-19 brought our entire planet to a screeching halt. Everything was canceled. Calendars were cleared. For the first time in our lives, most of us had nowhere to go (unless you were an essential worker, of course.)

At first, we kind of loved it. We appreciated this gift of time. We enjoyed the simple things in life, like taking walks around our neighborhood and having dinner around the table together. But after a few months of being stuck at home, we were over it. People started to get lonely and bored. We realized how much we craved human interaction, social events, and even a calendar to give us some sense of where we are in our world.

Dr. Ramon Solhkhah of the Jersey Shore University Medical Center said, "The pandemic has left many people feeling adrift because those daily routines that were essential to us before the COVID-19 crisis have evaporated and been replaced by uncertainty and a lack of structure that can contribute to stress, anxiety, and even clinical depression."[1]

Obviously, this is an extreme example of how we can feel out of balance by not doing enough things, but depending on your stage of life, it can happen anytime. If you don't have people to connect with, responsibilities to show up for, outlets to share your gifts with, or projects to plug into, you're going to feel bored and out of balance.

Reason #3: We're doing the wrong things.

My friend Eric hated his job, and his stress level and attitude were affecting every area of his life—his family, his friends, his faith, and especially his work. He stayed put because the benefits were great and the money was good, but when his wife finally talked to him about how he was snapping at everyone on an almost-daily basis, it hit him hard that he needed to make a change. He realized he was doing the wrong thing, so he began applying for other jobs.

It doesn't matter how much money you make. If you hate your job, you're going to feel out of balance. And the wrong things aren't just work-related. If you have responsibilities that suck the life out of you every single week, you're going to feel out of balance. If you have relationships that are toxic and drain you, you're going to feel out of balance. You can manage your calendar to be a perfect split between your work life and your home life, but if you're spending your time doing the wrong things, you're still going to feel out of balance.

> **You can manage your calendar to be a perfect split between your work life and your home life, but if you're spending your time doing the wrong things, you're still going to feel out of balance.**

Reason #4: We're not doing the right things.

Finally, the fourth way we feel out of balance is by not doing the right things. The right things are the things that are most important to us. So often, I hear people say things like, "I love to work out, but I never have time to." "I would love to go on a date with my spouse, but we can never make our schedules line up." "I want to play with my kids, but by the time I get home, I don't have the energy." If you don't spend time on the things that matter most to you, then of course you'll feel out of balance.

Take my friend Callie, for example. Even though she really wanted to go visit her dad who lived just ten miles away, Calli didn't make the time. Her life had gotten so busy with work, school, her kids' baseball and band practices, and an endless list of other responsibilities, that week after week went by without stopping by to see him. It wasn't intentional, of course. But she was just so . . . *busy.*

One day as she was driving around doing errands and knocking things off her to-do list like she always did, she thought about her dad. In that moment, she decided to put off being productive and drove to visit him right then. Sometimes the reason we have that nagging voice in the back of our minds telling us "this doesn't feel right" is because it *isn't* right. Even if we don't intend to, we focus on the wrong things—the less important things. We often pile on the responsibilities and tasks without asking ourselves if those are even important to us in the first place. And then we wonder why feel so out of balance!

When we do too many things or not enough things, when we do the wrong things or we don't do the right things, we will

> **Finding balance can be tricky because it isn't just a schedule problem; it's also a heart problem.**

always feel out of balance. But finding balance can be tricky because it isn't just a schedule problem; it's also a heart problem. Every commitment on our calendar and every task on our to-do list represents a deeper motivation inside of us. If we don't fix things at the root level and we only address our calendar, the problems will continue to creep up again and again. Whether we're doing too many things or the wrong things or maybe both, we need to get to the root of what's really going on in our heart.

FIVE TIME STEALERS

We can get to the root of our balance problem by identifying five time stealers we so easily fall into. On the surface, these five time stealers can seem harmless because they're normal needs we all feel from time to time. They aren't inherently bad, but if we aren't careful, they can lead to unhealthy patterns and habits that will run our lives into the ground. Just like a drug, they can be addictive. And because of the world we live in, that drug is always readily available. You may connect with some of these more than others, but let's explore each of them.

Time Stealer #1: The Need to Be Loved

I've always loved helping people. I genuinely love serving and supporting others. That's a very real part of my heart and who I am. As a Christian, I also believe that we are called to love and help others. This was the perfect explanation for why I felt run ragged for years, trying to do everything for everyone. I never wanted to say no. *I just love to help people so much! It's what I'm called to do!*

Then several years ago, I heard a pastor say something that has stuck with me ever since. He said, "There's a difference between doing something to be loving and doing it to be *loved.*" Ouch.

If I am truly honest with myself, a lot of my "helping" is really just an effort to be loved. I want other people to think I am nice and kind and a good person. I want people to like me. I want to be loved. This unhealthy need to earn love from others has driven me to say yes to things that were not important to me or even right for me.

I have been president of clubs I didn't care about, gone to events I didn't want to go to, and taken on projects that someone else could have, and probably should have, taken on. I once even volunteered to be a puppeteer for the kids' ministry at church. And to add insult to injury, that puppet was a rat! Every Sunday I hid behind a box making rat voices—not because I was called to serve, but because I was trying to earn love. The need to earn love from others can lead you to do too many things and the wrong things, leaving no room in your life for the right things.

Time Stealer #2: The Need to Impress Others

A friend was complaining to me a few years ago about how terrible she felt for sending her son to football practice in the wrong football pants. As she talked, I couldn't help but think about how little her son probably cared, which she admitted afterward. He just wanted to play football. The issue wasn't about whether or not he could practice in those pants. It was all about what the other moms thought of her.

Now with school-age children myself, I get it. Around every corner are comparisons over who has the perfect monogrammed backpack and who brings the best snack (organic, vegan, and gluten-free, of course!) to the class party. Parents are desperate to be the "good mom" or the "good dad" (translation: impressive), and we don't even realize the effect it's having on us.

I don't care what other people think of me! I think to myself as I'm up at midnight putting together the perfectly creative and thoughtful goody bags for my two-year-old's Pinterest-perfect party the next day. So why do we wear ourselves out trying to impress others with our attempts at perfection? We're holding ourselves to a standard that is exhausting at best and impossible at worst. And what's so sad is that by holding ourselves to this impossible standard of perfection, we inadvertently pressure others to hold themselves to it as well.

No one has it together, by the way. No one. Some might be better at covering up their mess than others, but we all have that one closet crammed with stuff we don't want anyone to see. This need to impress others is driving us to exhaustion and keeping us focused on insignificant tasks that our kids won't remember and no one even cares about.

Time Stealer #3: The Need to Prove Yourself

There's a scene in *A Few Good Men* where Demi Moore's character is telling Tom Cruise's character about her accomplishments, yet again. He pauses and then calls her out. "Why are you always giving me your résumé?" he asks. She looks a little embarrassed and then admits, "Because I want you to think I'm a good lawyer."

I've felt like that before. Haven't you? As I was coaching a business leader named Andrew years ago, I could tell he felt that pressure too. He was in the middle of taking over the family business from his dad, who had founded the company and run it for the past three decades. With a team of over fifty people, Andrew believed that everyone else thought he was only moving into the CEO role because of his last name. All day every day, he was weighed down by an intense pressure to prove that he deserved this title. He worked long days, seven days a week, but it didn't matter. He felt haunted by the fear that no one would respect him because the job was handed to him by his dad.

Whether you're a workaholic because you want to prove that you deserve a title or you're signing up to serve on every committee to show how committed you are, an unhealthy need to prove yourself will only drive you to overwork, overcommit, and overdo everything. But that black hole of insecurity can't be fixed by doing more. Because no matter how much you do, the lie that you're not worthy will still linger in the shadows, pushing you to prove yourself so you can earn your place in your own life.

> **That black hole of insecurity can't be fixed by doing more.**

Time Stealer #4: The Need to Feel Accomplished

My friend Nikki puts about forty-seven things on her to-do list every Saturday morning. As a mom of two with a full-time job, she only has the weekend to do everything on her list. The only problem, of course, is that she can't get forty-seven things done. Realistically, she probably can't even get seven of those things done—at least not if she wants to have any fun, rest, or family time.

And you know what? I've done the same thing. If I'm not careful, my to-do list can grow to about ten times what I'm actually able to accomplish in a given day. My need to check boxes and feel some sense of accomplishment leads me to be a cruel taskmaster in my own life. I pile the work on and then beat myself up when I don't get it all done.

Our obsession with checking boxes for some fleeting feeling of productivity becomes a vicious cycle that is incredibly hard to break. We're addicted to accomplishing things, even if those things are unimportant or irrelevant. When we try to do more things than we have time for, we will always feel out of balance. This unhealthy need to feel productive will keep us on a treadmill of to-do lists for the rest of our lives, and it will keep us from ever being able to enjoy rest, feel peace, or create balance.

Time Stealer #5: The Need to Escape

By the time my husband and I get home from work, feed our kids dinner, give baths, brush teeth, read books, and get three kids in bed, we are wiped. At that point, it's about 7:30 or 8:00, and all we want to do is crash. Our natural default is to sit on the couch and check out—to escape.

We might watch a show on Netflix or mindlessly scroll through social media on our phones, or maybe even both. Neither of those activities are bad, and we love watching a new show like anyone does. But if I'm honest, watching TV and scrolling on my phone isn't life-giving. Screens don't bring us closer together, they don't enrich our lives, and they don't make us better people. But because we're tired and often don't have the energy to think of something creative or different to do, we crash and check out. But it's not just us and it's not just in the evenings, either.

In fact, research shows that the average smartphone user touches their phone 2,617 times per day.[2] The average American spends about two hours and three minutes per day on social media and watches nearly four and a half hours of TV per day.[3,4] Screens aren't evil, but at the same time, I don't think any of us would say that Netflix and Instagram are the most important things in our lives. But if we're spending over forty hours a week on these outlets, while we claim to never have enough time for things we really care about, then it's worth digging into. We'll dive deeper into the addictive nature of technology later, but right now we need to realize that we're part of the problem too.

We have a need to escape. Yet there's a difference between watching a show every now and then to be entertained and crashing on the couch every night staring at a screen to escape. Without realizing it or meaning to, we can end up spending a lot of hours of our lives mindlessly staring at something we actually care very little about. If we aren't careful, we're going to know everything about everyone else's life but completely miss out on our own. Talk about being out of balance!

> **Without realizing it or meaning to, we can end up spending a lot of hours of our lives mindlessly staring at something we actually care very little about.**

THE STORIES WE BELIEVE

In June 2010, Brené Brown gave a TED Talk in Houston on the power of vulnerability. Her speech quickly went viral, and the idea of vulnerability caught fire. Everyone was talking about it. The truth in her words and teaching have set so many people free, including me. But over time, I've noticed a trend that has caused some people to adopt a narrative that not only isn't helpful, it's also just not true. But because this trend can be confused as vulnerability, we accept it and even brag about it. I see it on social media, hear it from friends, and even identify those voices in my own head at times. *I'm just a mess. I'm failing as a mom. Here's how I screwed up today. Here's where I blew it at work. I haven't had a shower in five days. I can't get it together.*

First of all, if you haven't had a shower in five days, please put this book down and go take one right now. Second, if we live in these narratives about how pitiful we are and how much we're failing, guess how we feel? Pitiful. Guess what we teach our kids? That we're failing. Guess what we teach others? That we're pitiful and failing. This is not an honorable humility and it's not a healthy vulnerability. This is self-deprecating, dishonest, and unhealthy thinking. True vulnerability is an incredibly powerful path that can lead toward personal transformation and connection with others. It is *not* where you adopt an identity about all the ways you think you're failing and choose to stay stuck there. We all make mistakes but that doesn't define who we are.

Just as time stealers can get us stuck, the stories or narratives we tell ourselves about who we are and how we're messing up can as well. If you believe that you're failing, you can't get it together, and you're a mess, then that is exactly what you will experience. And there's nothing about this thinking that feels desirable, much less balanced.

What If Things Were Different?

I met my friend Eve at a Young Life camp when I was in college. She was in charge of about twenty college girls, and she mentored us during the month we volunteered there. Eve is brilliant, loves God, and is loved by everyone who knows her. But my favorite thing about Eve is that she is comfortable in her own skin. She's at ease. I've never seen her wring her hands or scurry around.

Eve is secure in who she is and whose she is. And what's even more beautiful is that when you're with Eve, you're invited to do the same. She doesn't have to tell you to relax. Just by being around her, the tension releases from your shoulders and you begin to feel at ease. It's as if her mere presence is an unspoken invitation to rest in the beautiful truth of who you are. She's okay with who she is, and she invites you to be okay with who you are too.

> How much better would your life be if you stopped trying to earn people's love and instead rested in the truth that you are already loved?

How much better would your life be if you stopped trying to earn people's love and instead rested in the truth that you are already loved? How relieved would you feel if you could

29

stop striving to impress others and instead were able to be comfortable in your own skin? How much more margin would you have if you stepped off the treadmill of to-do lists because you understood that your worth didn't rely on accomplishment?

How much more fulfilled would you feel if you stopped escaping into a screen and began creating a life you didn't want to escape from? How much more pride and confidence would you feel if you rejected the narrative that you're always failing and started acknowledging and appreciating the ways you're succeeding? If you did all these things, how much more balanced would you feel, and more importantly, how much more would you actually enjoy your life?

I believe that you can do these things. And I believe you will. That's exactly what we're going to work toward together on this journey. We're going to create and cultivate a new version of balance. But before we go on, we need to first acknowledge that we live in a world that is very, *very* out of balance.

A Balanced Person in an Unbalanced World

My son Conley loves to play with little toy boats during his bath. He has one ferry boat that is big and blue and has lots of features on it. You can load cars onto it, and it even has little people that sit on the deck. The only issue with the ferry boat is that it sinks all the time. If water gets on the top, the boat sinks to the bottom of the tub. If you don't have the cars perfectly distributed on the platform, the boat tips over. At first glance, it looks like a really cool boat, but when you see that the slightest thing makes it sink, you realize it's actually not a great design at all.

Conley has another toy boat. It's simple and red. The design is nothing special, except for one amazing feature: it never sinks. The waves in the bathwater can toss and turn it, and it will continue to float. Conley can even hold it under water, but as soon as he lets it go, the boat shoots straight to the surface and flips upright again. It doesn't matter what comes against it, that little red boat always keeps its balance and stays afloat. Why? Because the boat itself is balanced. And that's my goal for you on this journey: to become a balanced person in an unbalanced world. Just because your world isn't balanced doesn't mean you can't be.

Our culture, workplaces, families, schedules, and lives are not perfectly balanced. And, realistically, they never will be. If all we do is work to fix and tweak those things, we will still feel out of balance. Sure, we might find some relief for a season, but as soon as our circumstances change, we will tip right over. But when we fix things within ourselves and work to become balanced, we can feel peace and joy and rest, even in the midst of a crazy world. We can be a balanced person in an unbalanced world who doesn't sink when problems come our way. We can stay afloat even during storms. And when someone tries to pull us down, which will happen, we can rise to the surface again.

YOU ARE INVITED

The day I took Carter to the pediatrician and learned that he had an ear infection instead of sore gums, we left with a prescription for an antibiotic. We got the prescription filled and started his medicine that night. Within a day or two, he was feeling great, and within a week, the ear infection was completely healed. Once we knew what the real problem was, we could find the right solution for it.

The same is true for me and you on our journey to finding balance in our lives. Now that you understand that balance isn't just a schedule issue but a heart issue too, you can do the work to find the right solution and become a balanced person in an unbalanced world. You can become a person who doesn't need to prove yourself, who has the courage to say no, and who stops chasing checked boxes. You can stop doing too many things, have the willpower to cut out the wrong things, and have the awareness to start doing the right things. You can create your own version of balance and begin to enjoy your life in a new way. And that's exactly what we are going to work toward in the pages ahead.

As a Christian, I know I can rest in God's purposes, promises, provision, and most of all, his peace. God wants us to have an *abundant life*: "I have come that they may have life, and that they may have it more abundantly" (John 10:10 NKJV). Don't you want that for yourself? I know I do. When you do the work you need to do, you will not only change your own life, but like my friend, Eve, you will invite others to do the same.

As I said in the introduction, at the end of each chapter you will have the opportunity to answer several journal questions and take a challenge. As you begin this journey of taking back control of your life and discovering what balance means for you, please don't skip this part of the book. Take the time to answer the questions in a journal or notebook and complete the challenges in your free digital Take Back Your Time Workbook. You can download this workbook at ramsey solutions.com/tbyt. You will find out so much about yourself, your struggles, your pain points, and your hopes in the process. Then you will be ready to create and live out your own version of balance.

JOURNAL QUESTIONS FOR REFLECTION

1. What part of this chapter stood out to you the most? What are your main takeaways from chapter 1?
2. What themes or patterns do you see when you look back on the last few years of your life? Is there a particular thing you struggle with again and again?
3. How have you tried to solve your problems with balance in the past? How did that work out for you?

Challenge: Your challenge for chapter 1 is to understand why you feel out of balance. Use the worksheet for chapter 1: *Understand Why You Feel Out of Balance* in your digital workbook at ramseysolutions.com/tbyt to guide you. Understanding this about yourself is going to help you know what you need to do as you move forward on this journey.

CHAPTER 2

THE PATH TO BALANCE

Matt and I used to have a dog named Rocky. Rocky's favorite thing in the world was to escape from our fenced backyard. We replaced our four-foot fence with a six-foot privacy fence, but Rocky still managed to jump over it. We even rigged "coyote rolls," these crazy things Matt discovered on YouTube one day, which involved running rope through PVC pipe and lining the top of the fence with it so Rocky couldn't grab on to the fence to jump over. It was exactly as attractive as you might imagine; it also did not work.

We are nice people and we took great care of Rocky, so I'm not sure why he wanted to get away so badly. But every time he did, it was the same routine. He would sit just outside the fence, staring at me . . . mocking me. I would call for him, but of course he would refuse to come. I would begin walking toward him, and he would sit perfectly still as though he was going to let me grab his collar and bring him back home. But as soon as I got about a foot from him, Rocky would dart off to a new spot where he would sit perfectly still, smiling with his tongue hanging out of his mouth. I would tell him to stay, walk to him as calmly as I could through gritted teeth, and the moment I got close again, he would dart off to another spot. The entire routine was not only exhausting, it was maddening! No matter how many times I tried and no matter how close I got to him, I felt like I would never catch him.

I think that's how a lot of us feel when it comes to achieving balance. Right when we think we have it figured out, things change. Just when we think we are getting close, balance evades us. We try to chase after it and that doesn't work. We try to tiptoe carefully and that doesn't work. We can never get there, no matter what we do. The whole thing *is* exhausting and maddening!

ARE YOU REALLY OUT OF BALANCE?

As we mentioned in chapter 1, life balance isn't about a 50/50 split between your work life and your home life, and it's not about doing everything for an equal amount of time. It's about doing the right things at the right time. But before we work to create a schedule and life that makes that possible, it's important to note that, although we may *feel* out of balance at times, it doesn't necessarily mean our entire lives are out of balance. Let's look at a few examples of how this can happen.

Tired Does Not Mean Out of Balance

When my alarm went off this morning, I could barely open my eyes. I was so tired, I couldn't move, and the thought of sitting up and swinging my legs off the side of the bed to actually stand seemed impossible. I was also tired last night when I had to drag myself back downstairs after putting three kids to bed to clean up the kitchen from dinner and make lunches for the next day. I was tired last week and last month too. I've been some level of tired off and on for pretty much the past six years since having my first child. If you are a parent, you know what this feels like. One year I was at my friend Erin's house a few weeks before Christmas. As we sat and talked, her daughter walked in the room and asked what she wanted for Christmas. Erin smiled at her daughter and answered, "A nap!" Isn't that the truth?! We can be tired, but if we're not careful, we can confuse *tired* with being out of balance.

But being tired doesn't necessarily mean your entire life is out of balance. Tiredness might be a symptom of a deeper issue

> **Tiredness might be a symptom of a deeper issue you need to address in your schedule and your life, or it might not. It might just mean you're tired.**

you need to address in your schedule and your life, or it might not. It might just mean you're tired. Maybe you had a late night or an early morning or you didn't sleep well in between. It might mean you're in an exhausting season of life where you're working more than usual, or it might just mean you need a nap. It's very hard to accurately assess your life when you're tired. You *might* be out of balance, or you might just be tired right now.

Stressed Does Not Mean Out of Balance

Lisa was facing a huge deadline at work, preparing year-end accounting records. She worked for a smaller company, so her role often looked more like two or three roles, especially during that time of year. She was working all hours of the day, even coming in on Saturdays just to get her work done. The stress was getting to her and she wasn't sleeping well. Her life felt overwhelming and out of control. Even though this was the pattern every year-end and Lisa knew in a few weeks it would all be over, it didn't keep her from questioning what was wrong with her life. Did she need to ditch her job completely?

Similar to being tired, it's hard to think straight when you're stressed. You feel worried, out of control, and anxious. You question everything, and it feels like what you're facing is something you'll have to face forever. If you're feeling stressed, that could be a symptom of a life that's out of balance, or it might just mean you're dealing with something really difficult right now. It might mean you have a tense situation at work, you're in a difficult season with one of your children, or you have a burden on your shoulders that you don't know how to handle. While none of that is fun, it doesn't mean your whole life is out of whack. You might just be stressed right now.

Overwhelmed Does Not Mean Out of Balance

Allison had just returned home from running to the grocery store. She hung her purse by the back door and looked around her house. Toys were on the couch, and couch cushions were on the floor. An entire puzzle was dumped on the living room rug. *I swear I just picked that up!* she thought. There were Gold-fish crumbs and discarded sippy cups and dinner still sitting half eaten on the highchair, booster seat, and floor.

As her eyes scanned the mess in front of her—the mess that was not there just twenty minutes earlier—she felt completely overwhelmed. *How can I clean nonstop, yet my house is still a disaster? Why do I put food on the table that is going to be complained about, spit out, and tossed on the floor? When am I going to get caught up and get it together? Why is my life such a mess?*

Whether you have a job that's overwhelming or a business that's overwhelming or a family that's overwhelming or are in a season of life that's overwhelming, we've all been there. But that doesn't mean your whole life is out of balance. It could be. It might be a sign that you need to change something about your life and schedule. But if you're just discouraged because right after you accomplish the amazing feat of putting all the laundry away, more dirty piles somehow appear out of thin air, that's okay. You're just overwhelmed. Laundry is overwhelming and life can be overwhelming. Your life might not be out of balance. You might just be a little overwhelmed right now.

So which is it? It's very difficult to see clearly when you're feeling tired, stressed, or overwhelmed. Your version of balance is going to look different in different seasons of your life, and that's okay. It should! If you're in a busy season at work leading up to a deadline, you are probably going to feel stressed and overwhelmed. Then once you're past that deadline, those feelings will level out. When you're going through a hard time, it feels like it will last forever, but it won't. You will get through it. and you will come out on the other side—probably stronger than you were before.

If you've been feeling tired, stressed, and overwhelmed all day, every day for months and years, then we will talk about how to make changes to improve your sense of balance in the coming chapters.

> **Don't let a bad day or a tough week make you believe that your entire life is out of balance.**

But don't let a bad day or a tough week make you believe that your entire life is out of balance. You may just need a long nap or a day off of work.

So how do we help control our feelings and create a sense of balance even while leading busy lives?

THE PATH TO BALANCE

One of the things that Apple has fine-tuned to an art is the set-up of their products. If you have any Apple products, you know exactly what I'm talking about. From the moment you pull that snug lid off the perfectly crisp white box, the device inside comes to life and *it* begins to teach *you* how to set it up. For example, I got Matt a set of AirPods Pro headphones last year for Christmas. These things are so crazy smart that when you put them in your ear, they run a diagnostic assessment called an Ear Tip Fit Test to see if they fit properly in your ears. Then they tell you what size rubber tips to use for maximum noise canceling. I'm sorry, what?

Now, contrast that experience with IKEA. I love IKEA. I do. I have several pieces of furniture from IKEA in my house. But there's a reason that entire businesses are dedicated to just putting together IKEA furniture. Their instruction manuals are supposed to be easy to understand because IKEA uses pictures instead of words. Except that the manuals are actually insanely difficult to understand because THERE ARE NO WORDS! *Is the stick figure facing right or left? Is that side of the shelf the finished side or the unfinished side? Is that screw the large one or the medium one or the tiny one or the very tiny one? Is there a sizing scale somewhere? WHAT AM I DOING?*

When you don't know the steps to complete something, it takes an already-frustrating situation and, amazingly, makes it *even more* frustrating. That's why I decided to take this elusive idea of balance and break it down into five simple steps. These five steps make up The Path to Balance that we are going to unpack in the pages ahead.

I've been teaching life balance at large events for over a decade, and I've also been living it out the best that I can in my own crazy-busy life along the way. I've boiled down all of my principles, practices, and habits into these five steps. This plan is not complicated or overwhelming. It is simple and it works. Let's look at a brief overview of the five steps in The Path to Balance before we dive into each of them in the coming chapters.

THE PATH TO BALANCE

Step 1: Decide What Matters

Step 2: Stop Doing What Doesn't Matter

Step 3: Create a Schedule That Reflects What Matters

Step 4: Protect What Matters

Step 5: Be Present for What Matters

Step 1: Decide What Matters

When we talk about life balance, what we are often referring to is time management. We want to feel good about how we spend our time and how we manage our schedules. The only problem is that it's really hard to see how things should be or could be when you're knee deep in the weeds of your own life. You're running kids from hockey practice to violin lessons to karate. You have back-to-back meetings all day sandwiched between a Bible study in the morning and a committee meeting at night. You're rushing to keep up but always have this feeling that you're coming from behind. How in the world are you supposed to figure out what balance means, much less create it, when you're running around like a crazy person?

That's why for the first step in The Path to Balance, I want you to take a moment and zoom out. Trying to change your schedule or clear your calendar isn't going to be enough. Instead, you need to get out of the weeds long enough to consider one important question: What matters most to you? Your answer to this question will inform the steps that follow and determine the schedule you create so that you can spend your one life on those things.

Step 2: Stop Doing What Doesn't Matter

Once you decide what matters to you, the next step on The Path to Balance is to stop doing what doesn't matter. This is where you ditch the distractions in your life. A distraction is anything that *isn't* important to you. These are things that we don't really care about in the grand scheme of things, yet we often spend a lot of time on them whether we realize it or not.

For example, you might be distracted by perfectionism or people-pleasing. Or you may be a member of four different committees or organizations but are only passionate about one of them. You may have a standing lunch date with an old friend who you have little in common with and are only meeting out of obligation. You might be distracted by social media like the entire rest of the world. Or you may perpetually volunteer for things you have no time for, like hosting Thanksgiving dinner—when your Aunt Sally, who loves to cook, would do a much better job and actually enjoys hosting. Those are just a few common examples; you probably have some others that come to mind.

So how do you know if something is truly a distraction? When you spend time deciding what matters to you in Step 1, you will have a new clarity in your life. What naturally happens next is that the things that don't matter become much more obvious.

Suddenly, you'll realize things you didn't notice before: *My iPhone just notified me that my total screen time last week was twenty-five hours! What? That's more than a day!*

Distractions not only steal time from things that are more important to you, but they also drain your energy and your joy. They breed resentment because you're spending your time, money, and attention on things you don't care about, which leaves no room for things that you do care about. In Step 2, you're going to identify everything in your life that's *not* important. These are the things that need to go. Distractions are a major source of stress and anxiety in your life, and when you get rid of them, you free yourself up to focus on what matters most to you and you get to actually enjoy your life. What a concept!

Step 3: Create a Schedule That Reflects What Matters

Dave Ramsey often says, "I can tell what you actually care about by looking at your bank account and your calendar, because that's where you spend your money and that's where you spend your time." Every time I hear him say those words, I have a gut check because I know that I'm not as intentional as I could be. Many of us aren't.

Many of us take a passive approach to our lives, which leads us to spend time on things that we don't actually care about. We react to opportunities and then feel resentful. We look at our calendar to see where we are supposed to be, never considering if where we're going is where we actually want to be. You'll never feel balanced if you continue to live your life this way. That's why Step 3 on The Path to Balance is to create a schedule that reflects what matters to you—the values you identified in Step 1. This schedule will reflect what is most important to you, and it will not include (or it will at least minimize) those things that are not important to you.

What's so exciting about this exercise is that you get to literally *take back your time*. You're no longer in the passenger seat. You're in the driver's seat. You get to call the shots and decide where your time is spent. Then, although you may still be busy at times, you will feel a sense of balance because you're no longer doing *everything*; you're doing the right things. You're doing the things that allow you to be the person you want to be and live the life you want to lead.

Step 4: Protect What Matters

When my friends Sam and Kate were first engaged and began planning their outdoor wedding, some people were appalled that they didn't want to get married in a church. They both grew up in the church and love church buildings. But they also both love the outdoors and felt more connected to God and his creation outside rather than in a building. It was their wedding, so of course it was their decision. But they were both shocked at how confused, even offended, some people were that the two of them weren't getting married where people thought they should. Some people asked passive-aggressive questions about it, and some close relatives directly told Sam and Kate that getting married in a church was "so important."

Isn't it funny how willing people are to tell you what should be important in your life? They really are. Everywhere you turn, someone is trying to pressure you or persuade you to think and act just like they do.

> **Everywhere you turn, someone is trying to pressure you or persuade you to think and act just like they do.**

Whether you're dealing with your wedding plans or your weekend plans, you have to learn to protect what matters. This is where you get to exercise your confidence muscle. Step 4 in The Path to Balance is all about setting boundaries, saying no, and protecting what matters most.

Step 5: Be Present for What Matters

After struggling with mom guilt for years, I had an epiphany one day. I realized that so much of the guilt I had been experiencing came from one consistent place: I always focused on where I was not. When I was at work, I was thinking about my kids and worrying if they were okay. When I was home with my kids, I was thinking about work and worrying about deadlines I was behind on. My mind was always where my body wasn't.

If you're always focused on where you're not, of course you're going to feel guilty. That's why the final step in The Path to Balance is to be present for what matters. Because it doesn't matter if you create the most perfect schedule in the world—if you aren't actually present for it, you miss it. You will show up to every event on your picture-perfect schedule but still be weighed down by guilt. We need to learn to be where our feet are. This means you truly engage with the people you're with and enjoy where you are right now. You aren't thinking about where you just came from or where you'll be later. The fifth step in The Path to Balance is to be present for what matters so you can truly experience, appreciate, and enjoy the life you're living.

A PROCESS YOU CAN REPEAT

One of my favorite devotionals is *My Utmost for His Highest* by Oswald Chambers. I've had this 365-day devotional for over fifteen years, and no matter when I pick it up to read it, the words on the page always hit me differently. I can read the same day every single year, but because my life has changed or I'm in a different season, the verses and lessons impact me in a new way each time.

The Path to Balance laid out for you in this book works in a similar way. This is a path you can revisit and repeat again and again as the seasons of your life change. What matters most to you in one season of life will be different than what matters most to you in another season. You may get married, have kids, change jobs, move to a new state, retire, or become an empty nester. These changes will shift what you want to focus on in that particular season. In fact, what matters most to you will probably change many times throughout your life, so it's important that you revisit these steps so you can create balance in every season of your life. We will talk about this more in the final chapter—chapter 8.

Throughout this book, I will give you practical examples and practices that you can implement along the way to help you make this path your own. I'm not going to tell you what balance should be for you, and I'm not going to define success for you. Instead, I am going to do what I believe good coaches do: I'm going to help you figure those things out for yourself and give you the tools you need to get there. This path will help you create *your* version of balance. It's your life after all. And that's the only version of balance that should matter anyway.

JOURNAL QUESTIONS FOR REFLECTION

1. Have you ever confused being tired, stressed, or overwhelmed with being out of balance?
2. When you read the overview of The Path to Balance, what stood out to you?
3. Which of the steps seems easy to you? Which ones seem like they might be hard?

Challenge: Your challenge for chapter 2 is to begin to define your version of life balance. This is an important step on this journey because you can't achieve something if you don't know what it is. Use the worksheet for chapter 2: *Define Your Version of Balance* in your digital workbook at ramseysolutions.com /tbyt to guide you. This is going to help you understand what life balance looks like for you so you can take the steps needed to create it as we move forward.

THE PATH TO BALANCE

Step 1: Decide What Matters

Step 2: Stop Doing What Doesn't Matter

Step 3: Create a Schedule That Reflects What
        Matters

Step 4: Protect What Matters

Step 5: Be Present for What Matters

CHAPTER 3

STEP 1:
DECIDE WHAT MATTERS

Katie Davis Majors has a very unusual life. After her high school graduation in 2007, when most of her friends were planning to head off to college, she was planning a move to Uganda, Africa. While there on a mission trip her senior year, she was asked by a local pastor to return to teach at his orphanage. It didn't take much to convince her, but she knew her parents would be a different story. She asked them if she could take a year off before college to go teach at the orphanage, promising to return after the year to attend nursing school. They finally gave in, and once Katie got there, she fell in love with the people and began dreaming up a ministry to feed and educate children in the community. As promised, she returned home after that year, but it didn't last long. She moved back to Uganda—this time for good.

Katie now lives in Jinja, Uganda, 7,000 miles from her hometown, is married, and has fifteen children, thirteen of whom she adopted while she was still single. Her days are spent doing things we can't even imagine—from rinsing beans to catching chickens for dinner to cleaning out a neighbor's hut. Meanwhile, she and her husband, Benji, run a nonprofit organization, Amazima Ministries, founded by Katie in 2008. Her schedule is unlike anything you've probably ever seen, and her time is spent in ways you and I may never understand. So how did that happen? How did this woman, now in her thirties, end up with *this* life?

I'll tell you one thing for sure: she didn't get here by looking at her calendar to see what she could fit in. She decided what mattered to her.

The first step on The Path to Balance is to decide what matters.

In a 2012 article published by Lifeway, Katie, now a *New York Times* bestselling author, said, "People ask me quite often why in the world THIS is what I have decided to do with my life." Her answer? "Because this is what makes my heart sing. . . . This is where I am happiest."[5] Katie responded to God's call and created a life that reflected the things that mattered most to her.

For me, being 7,000 miles from home in a foreign country with a unique culture, different language, and daily challenges definitely wouldn't be my idea of a happy place. But that's just the thing. When you're doing what you were created to do and being who you were created to be, it *is* your happy place. You can't imagine life any other way. It may seem crazy to someone else, but it's right for you. You're spending your life on the things that matter most to you. But how do you do that? How do you get to the place of knowing what those things are, like Katie did? That's what we're going to explore in Step 1 on The Path to Balance.

WHAT DO YOU WANT TO BE KNOWN FOR?

When you think about what you want to do with your life and time, what's important to you, and what matters most, you might feel a little stuck at first. You might feel a little overwhelmed with all the options. It might be hard to weed through everything you already have going on and look at your life with new eyes to discern what actually matters to you. That's why I want to start this step by asking you a slightly different question to get you there. Instead of first thinking about what matters to you, I want you to ask yourself this: What do I want to be *known* for?

For example, what comes to mind when you think about the name Oprah? What about Zig Ziglar or Dave Ramsey?

When I think of Oprah, I think about how generous she is. When I think of Zig Ziglar, I think of how positive he was. When I think of Dave Ramsey, I think of what a straight shooter he is. Chances are, you were thinking something similar for each of these people.

Why? Because each of those people has an incredibly strong and consistent reputation. You don't hear reports of Zig Ziglar being positive in one situation and a Debbie Downer in the next. You don't hear about Oprah being generous in one situation and stingy the next: *I'm taking your car and your car and your car!* You don't hear about Dave Ramsey being blunt with one caller on his radio show and beating around the bush with the next. *Well, I know you really want that new boat even though you have $100,000 in debt . . .* No. He'd probably say, *That's stupid! Don't buy the boat!*

These people have strong reputations because their actions and behaviors are consistent over time. They are known for something. The word *reputation* comes from the Latin word *reputationem*, which means "consideration." It's how people consider or label you—good or bad. All of us have a reputation, whether we realize it or not. The question isn't "Are you known for something?" It's "Are you known for what you *want* to be known for?"

If we aren't careful, we'll keep running around like crazy, doing things that create a life we don't want to lead and that make us into people we don't want to be. But when we think about what we want to be known for, we look at our lives differently. We zoom out of the day-to-day grind, our calendar and commitments, and we give ourselves permission to consider the type of people we want to be.

I was at an event recently and Pastor Craig Groeschel spoke on this very thing. He said: "While most people will ask, *'What am I going to do?'* I'm going to suggest you start with identity and instead ask, *'Who do I want to become?'* There's a big difference. It's not just focusing on actions. Start with identity because identity drives actions. In other words, when you know *who* you are, you'll know *what* to do."

> If we aren't careful, we'll keep running around like crazy, doing things that create a life we don't want to lead and that make us into people we don't want to be.

So what about you? Who do you want to become? What do you want to be known for? What do you hope people think of when they think of you? When you decide what kind of person you want to be, it brings your deepest values front and center in your life. And this is the starting place for helping you decide what matters most to you and what to do about it.

Leaving Labels and Limitations Behind

Notice that I want you to think about who you *want to be*, not who you think you *already are*. We make decisions differently when we think about it this way. When you think about who you *want to be*, you realize you have a choice in not only your actions but also your outcome. When you make decisions from who you think you *already are* (or are not), you might shrink back. You may play small and settle for some less-than version of yourself. Your actions show who you are, so when you change your choices, you will change who you are and what you're known for. You actually can become the person you want to be.

So, what does this look like in our everyday choices? Let me give you an example. Recently I was talking to my oldest son, Carter, about his sixth birthday coming up. As we were talking about what type of theme he wanted, he asked me if he could have—wait for it—a *squirrel* birthday.

My first thought was to say no. I was going to tell him to pick something else. Why? Because it was weird. Because they don't make squirrel birthday party supplies. Because I was tired. Because something else would be easier. Just because. But then I thought about it. I thought about what it would cost. Hardly anything. I thought about what it would take out of me. Not much. I thought about how cool it would be for a

58

six-year-old boy to have what he wants for his birthday. Pretty stinking cool. And I thought about the fun mom I *want* to be. So I said yes. I found some squirrel balloons on Amazon, made a ridiculous squirrel pinata and asked my mom (who happens to own a cake shop, conveniently) to make a squirrel cake for us. The whole thing was as weird as you are probably imagining. But you know what else? It was awesome.

Isn't it interesting how different the outcome is when we make decisions based on who we want to be instead of who we think we already are? We often say things like, "I'm not a fun mom." "I'm not a runner." "I'm not a businessperson." "I couldn't pull that outfit off."

Says who?

We do. And we do it all the time, don't we? We place labels and limitations on ourselves and then we live within them.

So the next time you find yourself living within some label you don't even like, ask yourself, "Says who?" Then, do something fun, run to the end of your street, put your idea out there, or wear that outfit. Then, *boom*! You are a fun mom. You are a runner. You are a businessperson. You pulled off that outfit. Your actions reflect who you are, so instead of accepting that you have to be someone you don't want to be, choose different actions. As George Eliot said, "It is never too late to be what you might have been."

I don't know what labels and limits you've been living within, but I want to remind you that you don't have to. You can break out of the box you've put yourself in and dream about something bigger and better for yourself, your life, and your future. I want to challenge you to reject all the labels and limitations, and I want you to believe that you really can be the person you want to be. And you can create the life you want to lead.

Who Do You Want to Be?

Let's put this into action. I want you to make a list of three to five words or statements that describe who you want to be. Grab a piece of paper or use the worksheet for chapter 3 in your free Take Back Your Time digital workbook—no, seriously, do it right now. These aren't necessarily the things that are most important in your life (for example, family, friends, faith, and so on), but rather, characteristics that show what you value most. This list will describe who you want to be and what you want to be known for. Again, this is not who you *think you are*; this is who you *want to be*.

Also notice that I said "three to five"—not thirty-five! You might be tempted to include everything that comes to mind. But the truth is, you can't be everything. Trying to be everything to everyone is one of the ways we get ourselves out of balance in the first place. As author and speaker Patrick Lencioni says, "If everything is important, then nothing is." You have to do the hard work of identifying what is truly important to you and narrowing down that list to an easy-to-remember list of three to five qualities.

I won't ask you to do anything that I'm not willing to do myself, so here is my list in full transparency and in no particular order. I want to be:

1. Hardworking
2. Generous
3. A Person of Integrity
4. Fun
5. Loving

These things reflect the type of person that I want to be and the qualities I want to be known for. Your list might include qualities like: present, empathetic, confident, rested, spontaneous, or kind. When you write out a simple list like this one, it's important because it will then help you decide what matters most to you.

WHAT MATTERS MOST

Deciding what kind of person you want to be is extremely important so you can make decisions in line with that. But your calendar probably doesn't have time slots for "hardworking" and "loving," right? Your calendar is full of commitments. Those commitments either reflect the qualities or values you listed or they don't. They are either moving you toward the person you want to be or away from it.

Before you create a calendar full of commitments that you actually care about, you need to get really clear on what those things are for you. To do that, you'll create another list: your What Matters Most List. For this, you'll think about what people, organizations, causes, activities, or commitments are most important to you. I'm going to give you some questions to help guide you as you start thinking of your list. Take a moment to write down your answers to these questions.

1. What do you **need** in order to be the person you want to be?

    Reflect on your list of qualities above. What helps you live out those qualities? For example, if I am going to be any fun, I need *rest*.

2. What makes you feel **balanced**?

    Think about when you feel the most balanced. What makes you feel that way? I feel balanced when I have quality time with the people I love the most—my family and friends. I also feel balanced when my house is (somewhat) clean and when I create time to exercise and grow in my faith each week. I don't have to spend time on everything, but I feel balanced when I spend time on those things.

3. What makes you come **alive**?

Recently, I was on stage for three days straight for our annual Business Boutique Conference. It was exhilarating and, as you can imagine, exhausting. I planned to rest as much as possible for the few days after, but then I remembered that I planned to make my son's Halloween costume for trick-or-treating that weekend. He wanted to be Waffle House. A server? No. A cook? Nope. Carter wanted to be Waffle House— the *building*. Obviously, this was going to take some time, effort, and creativity, but I was totally up for the challenge and thrilled to encourage his own creativity.

That Sunday evening after the conference, I got started on the costume and stayed up until almost midnight working on all the details, from the brick sides to the red awning to the yellow and black square logo. I didn't have to stay up that late, and I didn't even finish it that night, but I was having so much fun working on it, I didn't want to stop. Whether speaking on a stage or staying up late making a cardboard costume, using my gifts of creativity makes me light up and come alive. So, what makes you come alive? Those things are probably things that really matter to you.

As you think about your answers to these questions, the things that matter most to you should begin to become more clear. Now you're ready to write a list of what matters most to you. Try to keep this to under ten items, and don't worry about writing it in a particular order. Again, I'm going to do this with you so you see how this process progresses.

What Matters Most List

As I sat down to write my What Matters Most List, I looked back at my answers to the questions above and copied those down in list form. Then I added and changed a few things to get to my final list. This is what matters to me and makes me feel balanced. Here it is:

1. Quality time with my children and husband (together and separately)
2. Exercise
3. My faith
4. Rest
5. Play
6. A (somewhat) clean house

7. My work
8. Alone time
9. Friendships
10. Creative outlets

Now, it's your turn. Write your own What Matters Most List. These are the relationships, activities, and commitments that make you light up and come alive. When you spend time on these things—the right things—you feel balanced. They are the things you need in your life to be the person you want to be. Once you have your list, it's going to help you know what values you want to live out in your day-to-day life. But as we all know, even if you have a list of seven to ten things that are important to you, you can't do them all, all the time. You have to prioritize.

THE PROBLEM WITH PRIORITIZING

While in college, I was mentored by a woman named Jana. Even though 99 percent of our relationship was Jana pouring into me, there was one moment when I was actually able to help her. She was feeling overwhelmed and stressed by all the things she was juggling, and as she told me about it, I had a lightbulb moment.

I grabbed a piece of paper and a pencil and said, "Jana, it seems like this is how you see your life." I drew two horizontal lines with several vertical lines connecting the horizontal ones like a ladder. Then I filled in the boxes with different areas of her life.

Husband	Girls	Church	Bible Study	Friends	Work

I said to Jana, "God is obviously always first in your life, but after that, it seems like everything else is on the same level. When two things in your life compete, you have a hard time making a decision between the two. So, for example, if I wanted to have lunch with you on your husband's birthday, you would feel torn about what to do."

Then I drew a pyramid with several horizontal lines. "But I see my life like this . . ."

"My family comes before friends. So if you wanted to have lunch with me on a day when my mom is in town, I wouldn't even have to think about my answer. I'd say no and spend the day with my mom." This was also a lightbulb moment for Jana. She understood why she was feeling so overwhelmed. She wasn't necessarily doing the wrong things. She just hadn't been prioritizing all of the right things.

Like Jana, when we treat everything in our lives as equal, we feel stressed and anxious. We have a hard time making decisions and we feel guilty when we actually do. We have a problem with prioritizing. Even if you're not doing *too* many things and even if you're not spending your time on the *wrong* things, you still have to be able to prioritize the *right* things.

Everything Is Not a Priority

I'd love to say that prioritizing has always been easy for me, but it hasn't. It's really hard. And more than that, I think it tends to be especially hard for women. In their book *Men Are Like Waffles—Women Are Like Spaghetti*, Bill and Pam Farrel say that men's brains tend to operate more like waffles with very distinct compartments, while women's brains seem to function more like spaghetti with everything tangled together.[6] Neither is right or wrong—just different. But it does show why I, and many women, struggle to prioritize—and why *everything* feels like a priority.

My coworker told me a story of how this plays out in his marriage. On a Sunday morning, for example, his goal is to get the family out the door to church. That's it. That's his one priority. His wife, on the other hand, wants to get the family out the door to church *and* sweep the floors (*just real quick before we leave*) *and* start the crockpot (*so we have something to eat for dinner*) *and* throw in a load of laundry (*we have nothing clean!*) *and* gather the dry cleaning to drop off (*might as well while we're out*). To her, there is no hierarchy of priorities; everything is equally important. He wonders why she is running around trying to do all of those things when all their family really has to do is get to church. She wonders why he isn't helping! *Hurry up! Get your dirty work shirts so we can drop them off while we're out!*

The definition of *prioritize*, according to the *Oxford English Dictionary*, is to "determine the order for dealing with (a series of items or tasks) according to their relative importance."[7] And for many of us, that's very hard to do. We treat everything as if it's equally important, and we have a very hard time letting things go. Instead of cutting things out, we multitask to try to make it all fit. Instead of prioritizing what's most important, we stress ourselves out treating it all as important. We are obsessed with productivity, so we can do more in the same amount of time. But our goal on this journey to balance isn't about how to do more of everything. It's about how to prioritize—and actually enjoy—the right things.

Your time, money, and energy are finite. You're always going to have to make choices. You can either make choices that reflect what matters most to you, or you can try to do it all and fail. Because you will. You can't do everything you want to do. And you certainly can't do everything everyone else wants you to do. The needs, opportunities, and demands of your life will always exceed your ability to meet them. We are painfully limited in what we can fit in.

> The needs, opportunities, and demands of your life will always exceed your ability to meet them.

But you get to choose. You can try to do everything and feel like a failure when you don't—because you won't. Or you can intentionally choose what you focus on and what you let go of. You can stop feeling like a victim and realize that the person in charge of you is you. Or as Shelley Giglio said, "Some days I feel like my life is too much. Then I remember that I am in control of my yes."

You are in control of your yes. You are the person in charge of your calendar, your household, your energy, and your stress.

You can set yourself up for success. You can realize that everything is not important and prioritize what actually is.

What Makes the Cut

My whole house is never clean at the same time. Unless we are all out of town and a magic fairy comes by to clean it while we are gone, it just doesn't happen. Now I could look at that and feel really guilty about it. I could focus on all the rooms that need to be picked up and I could feel bad about myself for the things left undone. Or I could do something different, which I do. I choose the mess. What does that mean? It means I intentionally choose which parts of the house I fight to keep clean and I choose which parts of the house I let go.

For me, the rooms that I want to work hard to keep clean are the kitchen, living room, and our bedroom. I spend the majority of my time in those rooms so I want them to be clean. As for the playroom, the kids' rooms, and the deck? I just let those go. The kids are going to drag out their toys the moment I clean those areas anyway, so what's the point? I may pick them up once every week or two, but I don't stress myself out over it. The rooms that matter to me make the cut and those that don't, don't.

This small change—choosing what to fight for and what to let go of—has been revolutionary in how I see my home . . .

and myself. Now when I walk into the bonus room and it looks like there has been a toy explosion, I don't feel like a failure. I feel in control because I am. I chose that mess.

Could I spend every evening cleaning and picking up every room before I go to bed? Probably. But that's not how I want to spend my time, and that's not how I want to spend my life. I want to spend my evenings with my children before they go to bed, and I want to spend the time after that with my husband. I don't want to spend my time picking up toys in rooms that no one sees and that my kids will just be playing in again the next day. That mess represents time better spent somewhere else, and I don't beat myself up for it.

The good news is that you can do this too. You can do this with your house, and you can do this with your life. You can decide what you fight for and what you let go of. You decide what makes the cut on your calendar and what doesn't. You can, maybe for the first time in your life, prioritize. You get to decide what makes the cut.

Fixed and Flexible Priorities

When most people think of priorities, they think of things that are static and set in stone. For example, someone might say, "My priorities are God, family, others, and self, in that order."

That's a nice Sunday School answer, but it's not all that helpful for real-life time management.

It's important to have fixed priorities so you know how to make decisions if all heck is breaking loose. But this list of fixed priorities is impractical when it comes to actually creating your calendar.

That's why you also need flexible priorities. Flexible priorities are more specific than your fixed priorities, and they will reflect your season and situation. They may change as your situation changes and your focus shifts. You will have several versions of flexible priorities—priorities for this season, priorities for this week, and priorities for each day.

Priorities for This Season

As you think about your flexible priorities, you need to consider the season you're in. If you have a big project or a major deadline at work, your focus for that season would be work. Then in a different season, your focus might shift to family to take care of an ailing parent or maybe a child who is struggling in school.

If you set a new goal in one of the areas that is important to you, such as running a half marathon, then exercise and training would move up on the priority list for that season.

Your priorities in any season should reflect what matters most to you at that time. Everything can't be equally important all of the time, so you're going to shift your priorities based on what's going on right now in your life.

For example, this fall I have been crazy busy working on this book, my show, and the Business Boutique event. Work is at the top of my priorities in this season and my calendar reflects that. I haven't been exercising, resting, or cleaning as much as usual. I have spent the majority of my time working and with my family. Those are the priorities from my What Matters Most List that I am focusing on in this particular season and how I spend my time reflects that.

Think about this for yourself right now. What are your top priorities in this current season? Use your Take Back Your Time Workbook at ramseysolutions.com/tbyt to make your list on your worksheet for chapter 3.

Priorities for This Week

Within each season you will get even more specific and identify priorities for each week. Those priorities might be right in line with your priorities for this season or they may be different that week. That's okay. For example, even though I'm in a season of focusing on work, a couple of weeks ago looked a little different. Since I had just wrapped up my three-day event, I had an easier work week the week following. I took Monday off to take my husband to breakfast for his birthday, and I spent my evenings working on the crazy Waffle House costume for my son. I also had doctors' appointments for me and my kids, and I cleaned up around the house to play catch-up. I was still in a season of focusing on work, but that particular week looked different as I focused on family, creativity, and cleaning.

At the beginning of each week, write down what you want to focus on for that week. The priorities you set for the week can and should reflect what is most important to you at that time. The priorities you plan for each week are more current, relevant, and specific than the priorities for this season. Try this for yourself. What are your top priorities for this week? Write them down.

Priorities for Each Day

In addition to having priorities for each season and each week, you can have another, more detailed list for each day. No two days are ever the same, so it helps to know what is most important before your day begins.

Start each day by deciding what you want that day to look like. Make a list of what your priorities are going to be for that specific day. These are the things that you want to focus on the most. We will talk more about how to use this list of priorities to plan your day in chapter 5.

I like to think before the day begins, *If I get nothing else done today, I want to get* this *done.* This helps me decide in advance how I want to shape my day. It keeps my day from getting derailed and helps me feel that I have accomplished what I want to get done the most. For example, my top priorities today are:

1. Finish chapter 3 of my book
2. Swap out summer and winter clothes from the attic
3. Go out on a date with Matt

As you get more specific with your daily priorities, keep in mind that every single item you prioritize might not be listed on your original What Matters Most List. As you can see above, work and alone time with my husband are reflected in this list, but swapping out seasonal clothes is just something I have to get done. It doesn't make me light up and come alive, but it is a priority if I want my family to stay warm this winter.

As you get more specific with your priorities, your daily and even weekly priority lists will likely get more tactical and practical than your original What Matters Most List. Your daily list will also reflect the most current, relevant things going on with you each day. When things come up, and they always do, they get integrated into this daily list. Try this exercise one more time to practice. What are your priorities for today? Write down your top three to five items on a piece of paper.

Priorities are not a "set it and forget it" type of thing. Your season, week, and day will inform what matters most to you. This helps ensure that you are doing the right things at the right time. Get in the habit of deciding what your priorities are for each season, each week, and each day. Then write them down to make sure you're focusing on what matters most to you. Writing them down is also going to help you create your calendar in Step 3. Use the worksheet for chapter 3 in your Take Back Your Time Workbook to guide you.

When Priorities Change

There will be times when your priorities need to change because your situation has changed—either *by* you or *for* you. For example, let's say you have plans to go on a vacation with your spouse and that is the priority for May. You've arranged childcare and budgeted the money. You've taken off work and moved everything in your life around to make that happen. Then you find out your mom has an alarming medical diagnosis and needs you. Suddenly your priorities change. You're canceling flights and hotels and rearranging your life to reflect the new priority: your mom. A shift in priorities may affect your week or it may affect your year, but the key is to be able to adjust what is important to reflect the change.

Then there are times when your priorities may just change for a day. You might start your day planning to be home by 5:30 p.m. so you can have dinner with your family. But then you get a call that your boss needs to have an urgent meeting with you at 5:00. This means you won't make it home on time. Your priorities shift to make the meeting.

Of course, if this happens every day, that's a problem. But when things come up—and they always do—you can be flexible and adjust. You don't need to feel guilty or beat yourself up for changing your mind, your priorities, and your plans. You can set priorities for the season you're in, your week, and even each day. And when you need to change them, which you likely will, you can be okay with doing that as well.

Priorities Require Focus

If you are still having trouble staying on track even after you prioritize, you may not have a prioritizing problem but, instead, a focusing problem. Both involve making a choice of one thing over another, and let's be honest, sometimes we just don't want to choose. We want to do everything all the time and *it's all important*! But believing everything needs to get done is keeping you from getting anything done. You feel scattered because you are. You can't make progress because you can't stay focused.

Focus is critical to sticking to your priorities. It creates momentum, and momentum creates progress. If you want to reach a new goal, you have to learn to focus. If you're going to make a change, you're going to need to focus. If you're going to do anything, it's going to take focus!

> Believing everything needs to get done is keeping you from getting anything done.

For example, millions of people have gotten out of debt and changed their lives with our *Financial Peace University* class at Ramsey Solutions. These people are able to do that by focusing on what is most important to them: paying off their debt. That focus drives them to cut back on expenses, pass on eating out with friends, give up vacations, and find ways to earn extra income. The result is that the average family who goes through the class pays off $5,300 of debt and saves $2,700 within the first 90 days. How does that happen? Focus.

Dave Ramsey says, "You can wander into debt, but you *can't* wander out." And that is the truth! When these people reach their goal, they celebrate by eating out and taking vacations. But when paying off their debt is their top priority, they focus to make it happen. They say no to less important things so that they can say yes to the most important thing.

The same is true for you. If you want to treat your priorities like the most important thing, you have to actually focus on them. If you want to finish that house project or land that new client or have a better relationship with your spouse, you're going to need to focus on that priority for it to actually happen.

HOW TO BE A TEAM

If you're married or have children, then you already know all too well that your life isn't just about you and what you want. If anything, you probably feel last in line and lost in the mix of your many roles and responsibilities! I don't want you to live in the extreme of feeling lost in your own life, but in your search for balance, you also don't want to steamroll everyone in your path either. Your life is shared with others, and balance will be too.

Balance won't be possible for anyone in your family without everyone in the family being on board. It's important to have a conversation about what matters to you with the people you share your life with. As you consider what's important to you, ask your spouse and your children what is important to them. Let this spark a conversation that allows everyone to be seen and heard. You can even take it a step further and invite each person in your household to write their What Matters Most List and priorities as well.

When you have a family, your time is not just your time; it's your family's time also. You are a team, and to be a team, you need to be working toward the same goal. Invite your family into this journey and exercise with you. Then, when you begin to create a calendar, they will be ready and able to speak into that as well.

DEFINING SUCCESS

Often, one of the reasons we never feel successful in our search for balance is simply because we never define it. We run harder and do more, hoping to achieve some elusive version of success. But the finish line always moves and we never get there. We fill our lives so full and still feel empty. We work really hard but end up creating a life we don't even want. We do things we don't enjoy with time we don't have to impress people we don't even like!

If you want to achieve balance in your life, you need to define what that means *to you*. You need to define your finish line and identify what success looks like *for you*, and specifically what it looks like for you in this season. How can you be the person you want to be? How can your life reflect what matters most to you? If you don't begin with the end in mind, you will end up crossing someone else's finish line. And worse, you'll work really hard for a life you don't actually want.

So what does success look like for you when it comes to balance? Now that you've thought about what you want to be known for, captured what matters most to you, and even practiced prioritizing those things, think about how that informs your version of balance in this season of life. This will help you know what you're working toward on the rest of this journey.

> If you don't begin with the end in mind, you will end up crossing someone else's finish line. And worse, you'll work really hard for a life you don't actually want.

YOU GET TO CHOOSE

I recently spoke to our company on life balance. I asked the audience to do what I've asked you to do in this chapter. I asked them to think about what they want to be known for and to decide what matters to them. Then I challenged them to write those things down. After my talk was over, I was standing near the stage talking to some of my coworkers. A man named Bill, who I had met before but didn't know well, came up to me and shyly asked, "Can I talk to you?" I said yes and stepped aside so we could have some privacy.

Bill began to tell me his story of what he had gone through in the past year. Betrayal in his marriage. Heartbreak. Divorce. Single-parenting his two young children. His voice shook as he fought back tears and said:

> I was in church one day after all of this started, and I felt God asking me to write down a list of qualities describing the man I want to be. I need you to know that I'm not like that. I'm not a super spiritual person, and I definitely don't "hear" from God, whatever that means. But for some reason, I took out a small scrap of paper and wrote down five words that I want to be. I folded up the paper and put it in my pocket. I had no idea when I wrote those words on the page that day how much I would need them. I had no idea how devastating and difficult the months to come were going to be. But it was this list that carried me through. It was these words that kept me centered and focused

on who I want to be. When my wife would do something terrible, I didn't react how I wanted to. Instead,
I looked at this list and acted based on the man I want
to be. It has helped me in more ways than I could have
ever imagined at the time.

Bill reached for his wallet and pulled out a small, worn
piece of paper with five words on it. As he held it up for me, I
fought back the tears myself.

Bill's story is such a powerful reminder that we get to
choose. You and I get to choose who we want to be in this life. I
don't want you to get to the end of your life having missed what
mattered the most and wishing you'd lived true to yourself—
and true to who God has created and called you to be. Instead,
I want you to think about this and pray about this so that you
can decide who you want to be, what matters most to you, and
what kind of life you want to lead. Once you know that, then
you can start to actually make it happen.

JOURNAL QUESTIONS FOR REFLECTION

1. What do you sense God is teaching you about yourself based on your list describing who you want to be and what matters most to you?
2. How did you feel about prioritizing based on your season, week, and day? Was that easy or hard?
3. What does balance look like for you in this season of life specifically?

Challenge: Your challenge for chapter 3 is to decide what matters and prioritize it. Use the worksheet for chapter 3: *Decide What Matters (and Prioritize It!)* in your digital workbook at ramseysolutions.com/tbyt to write your lists and help you put into practice everything you learned in this chapter.

CHAPTER 4

STEP 2:
STOP DOING WHAT DOESN'T MATTER

I don't have anything to wear. No, seriously. I don't. I have a closet full of clothes but nothing to wear. Some of the clothes are too small and some are too ugly. Some have stains and some have snags and tears. Some are out of season or out of style. And others . . . well, I'm just over them.

I'm willing to bet you've felt the same way before. You stand there staring at your closet, sliding hangers to the right and to the left, overwhelmed with so many unexciting options. The truth is that I *do* have things to wear. But when my closet is stuffed with clothes I don't wear and don't like, I start to feel like that's all I have. The good options are so covered up by bad options that the bad eclipses the good. I completely forget that I do have things I actually like; I just can't find them in all that clutter!

This is when I know it's time to purge my closet. It's actually one of my favorite things to do. It's so rewarding and motivating—like free therapy. I love the "if you haven't worn it in a year, it has to go" rule. If I didn't have that rule, I'd never get rid of anything. If you've never purged your closet, you may be one of those people who thinks, *I'll just hold on to this. Who knows? Maybe I'll wear it again someday.* Chances are, if you haven't reached for that shirt since 1997, you're not going to this week either.

Many of us let our closets fill up with things that aren't right for us anymore, and we hold on to clothes and shoes well past their season. And you know what? We do that with our schedules too. We end up with schedules full of stuff—so much stuff that we can't see what's right for us anymore. We go to appointments and commitments and practices and meetings, then we drag ourselves to bed at night saying the same thing: "I have no time."

The second step on The Path to Balance is to stop doing what doesn't matter.

The truth is, you do have time. You just have to get rid of the clutter so you can actually see it. It's time to purge things from your calendar like you purge clothes from your closet.

That's why Step 2 on The Path to Balance is to stop doing what doesn't matter to you. In the last chapter, you decided what matters most to you. Now that you know what's important, it's time to get rid of everything that *isn't* important. These are all the distractions in your life, and it's time to ditch them.

WHAT IS A DISTRACTION?

A distraction is anything that isn't important to you. These are the *wrong* things that I mentioned in chapter 1. If you want to create balance in your life, you have to cut out the crap that's stealing your time and your joy. Distractions keep us stuck on the hamster wheel, always running and feeling like we don't have any time. But if we cut out some of these distractions, we will have the time we need to spend on the things we want. We will also have a lot more energy for those things! Now let's talk about some of the most common distractions in our lives so that we can start ditching them.

Distraction #1: Making Other People's Problems Your Problem

Several years ago I got an email from the YMCA, notifying me that there wasn't a coach for my four-year-old son's soccer team. *I know!* I thought. *I'll do it! I played soccer most of my life and coached my little sister's team. I can totally do this!*

I was five months pregnant at the time and working hard to prepare for my upcoming maternity leave. I could fill the rest of this book with all the reasons volunteering to coach the team was a terrible idea, but at the time I didn't think about whether or not it was a good idea. I just reacted. I made someone else's problem my problem. And over the next few months, as I was organizing who brought the oranges to practice each week and stressing over canceling the game when it rained in forty-degree temperatures in February, I paid for it. It didn't help that it turned out my son actually hated soccer. At every single practice and game, he would cling to my leg under my big pregnant belly and beg, "Mommy, can we please go home now?" *I wish!*

Whether you're a natural problem solver and can't restrain yourself when you see a need or you feel it's your duty to be a "good Christian," "good mom," "good whatever," you are allowing yourself to be distracted by other people's problems, which leaves less room to deal with your own problems. And none of this helps create balance in your life.

I know you want to help, but making everyone else's problems your own problems suggests you might struggle with boundaries. Obviously, I can relate. I love the book *Boundaries* by Henry Cloud and John Townsend. In it, Cloud writes, "Boundaries define us. They define *what is me* and *what is not me*. A boundary shows me where I end and someone else begins, leading me to a sense of ownership."[8]

Think of it like a yard around a home. If you have a yard, more than likely you know where its perimeter is. You know which grass you are responsible for and which you aren't. Your neighbors know this as well. How would you feel if you walked out your front door one day and your neighbor was on their hands and knees pulling all your weeds? You would feel weird, right? Maybe thankful, but probably weird. That's what it's like when we make everyone else's problems our problems. It's like feeling responsible for the weeds in your neighbor's yard when you have your own weeds to deal with!

> **You can and should be there for people and help those in need, but you shouldn't feel obligated to fix every problem that crosses your path.**

You can and should be there for people and help those in need, but you shouldn't feel obligated to fix every problem that crosses your path. You don't have to play the hero or savior.

Ditch the distraction of making everyone else's problems your problems. Instead of reacting to situations, take the time to think about whether something is right for you. We will talk about how to do this more in the next chapter so you can ask better questions before you commit to something. Then you will know you are helping with what really matters to you and in a way that honors everyone involved.

Distraction #2: Focusing on the Wrong Thing

Two years ago, I was trying to get a Christmas photo of our entire family, all in matching red pajamas, all looking at the camera and smiling. I am a very determined person, so even though Carter was pulling ornaments off of the tree behind us and Conley was climbing on my head, choking me with the neck of my shirt, I didn't give up. We tried about 4,657 times to get a good photo. And guess what? We didn't get a single normal one.

After that exhausting and very sweaty experience, I realized something. I wasn't focused on having a fun night with my family, playing games, and being silly. I was focused on getting a photo of it. I wanted a perfect photo to remember that night and how fun it was, and of course, to post on social media. In an effort to capture what a fun night it was, I created a situation that was the complete opposite of fun: a moment full of stress, sweat, and tears. All for a stupid photo. I was focused on the wrong thing and almost ruined our night.

That experience was so similar to a scene from the show *Little Fires Everywhere* that Matt and I watched recently. It's an incredibly powerful story, but there's one scene where Elena, played by Reese Witherspoon, tries to get a family photo for their Christmas card. Everyone is wearing coordinating outfits with plaid accents that Elena purchased and demanded everyone put on. One of her daughters, Izzy, doesn't want to wear the plaid shoes her mother bought, and it leads to a stand-off screaming match in front of everyone, including the photographer. When I watched this scene, as dramatic as it was, I couldn't help but see myself in Elena. I don't want to be anything like that, yet I do things like that. This is what happens when we focus on the wrong thing.

While I still love to have pictures of my kids all looking at the camera and smiling for special occasions, I don't obsess over it. Now I try three times to get a picture and then we move on. That way the focus is on actually *enjoying* what we're doing instead of *capturing* what we're doing. I reset my expectations for pictures and actually enjoy my life and my kids more now. Whether it's obsessing about a family photo or demanding your middle-schooler wear their shirt tucked in at church or counting every single calorie, focusing on the wrong thing will steal your joy. It will not only distract you from what really matters, but it will sabotage your ability to feel balanced.

We have to ditch the distraction of focusing on the wrong thing. Instead, we should remind ourselves of what matters most to us and then make decisions according to that. When we do this, we'll have more time for what matters, more real pictures, and more fun.

Distraction #3: Overdoing It

You may have heard the quote, "If it's worth doing, it's worth overdoing." As ridiculous and funny as it is, I have to admit that it hits home with me as a Type A go-getter. That's the reason I commit to way more than I can actually do with work, and it's the reason I always have way too much food for every party I host. Everything in my life follows the pattern of *more equals better*. But more doesn't always equal better. Sometimes more is just . . . more. More clothes in your closet than you can wear and more commitments on your calendar than you can keep up with. More responsibility than you want, more tasks on your to-do list than you could ever do, and more headaches than you have medicine for. More is not better. It's just more, and in many cases, it makes life harder and more complicated.

Take Cory for example. He was a newbie at his company. Having just finished his college degree, he was hired after a friend of his referred him for a position. Cory was sharp and wanted to prove himself to his peers and leaders—so much so, that he started to grate on everyone's nerves. Whenever his boss asked for a volunteer to work on a project, Cory was the first to raise his hand. In meetings, he was always one of the first to speak up. He would jump in front of other people to do anything and everything, and although he wasn't *trying* to be annoying, he was. He felt a desperate need to prove himself in his new position because he feared people wouldn't think he deserved it.

So much of our drive to overdo things comes from a need to prove ourselves worthy—whether that's for a job, a person, or something else. We go the extra mile, and then we go a few more just for the heck of it. We desperately want people to believe that we deserve our place in life, and we do everything we can to earn it. We fill our calendars with commitments that run us ragged, but we don't enjoy any of them. We have a full life, but it's not fulfilling.

Friend, you don't have to strive so hard. You are enough. I know you've heard that before, but you may not believe it. You don't have to go above and beyond. You don't have to go the extra mile. You don't have to overdo everything to earn your spot in your own life. You don't have *anything* to prove.

You are enough as a parent. You are enough as a friend. You are enough as a leader. You are enough, even in all your imperfections, just as you are. You are enough because God says you are. You are enough in him. When you quit trying to pull yourself up by your bootstraps to show the world you are good enough, you might actually realize you already are. And you always were. Ditch the distraction of overdoing it and allow yourself to relax in the powerful truth that you have nothing to prove.

> **When you quit trying to pull yourself up by your bootstraps to show the world you are good enough, you might actually realize you already are. And you always were.**

Distraction #4: Doing Things to Feel Productive

Did you know that slot machines make more money than the film industry and baseball combined, even though they only cost a few quarters at a time?[9] How is that possible? Because they make you believe you aren't spending much at all. A few quarters here, a few there. You insert such a small amount of money at a time that you don't notice how much you're actually losing . . . or how addicting the machines are.

The same is true for our to-do lists. There is something not only rewarding but addictive about checking off boxes. One task here, one there. And when all the items on our to-do list have been accomplished, what do we do? We add more. In fact, we are so addicted to the feeling of accomplishment that if we do something that is *not* on our list, we take the time to go back and put it on the list so that we can check it off! Why do we do that? One word: dopamine.

When we check boxes that show we have been productive, we get a dopamine fix. Dopamine is the chemical your brain releases when you do something that gives you pleasure. That "fix" causes you to want to repeat the behavior. Whether it's eating candy or checking boxes, your brain is telling you to do that more. It's operating in the reward center of the brain. According to *Psychology Today*, this chemical can lead us to repeat behaviors whether they benefit us or not:

> In lab experiments, dopamine prompts a rat to press a lever for food again and again. This is no different in humans; it's the reason why we partake in more than one helping of cake. This press-the-lever action applies to addiction as well. . . . Dopamine creates reward-seeking loops in the sense that people will repeat pleasurable behavior, from checking Instagram to taking drugs.[10]

Most of us know that social media and technology are addictive, but have you thought about something as seemingly innocent as your to-do list? We fill it with forty-seven things every Saturday, and we never get through it all. If by some miracle we do, we don't celebrate and relax; we pile on more. And for every item we actually need and want to accomplish on our list, we put about nine more things that we don't really have to do. Our lists are filled with essentials like "pay bills" and nonessentials like "steam-clean couch cushions." No wonder we feel out of balance. We're spending our finite time on the treadmill of to-do lists and there's no end in sight.

Having a to-do list can be an invaluable tool and an effective process for getting things done. But if you aren't careful, you will spend your entire life checking boxes and never stop to ask yourself if those boxes represent anything worth doing. I don't

> **If you aren't careful, you will spend your entire life checking boxes and never stop to ask yourself if those boxes represent anything worth doing.**

know about you, but I don't want to spend my life as a slave to my to-do list. I like what John Mark Comer says in his book *The Ruthless Elimination of Hurry*: "What you give your attention to is the person you become."[11] I want to spend more time being present with people and spend less time rushing through errands and tasks. I want to be productive, just like you do. But I don't want to do just anything. I want to do the right things. We're going to talk about how to do that in the next chapter because a to-do list that doesn't create the life you want is the wrong list. Change how you do things and you can change your life.

Distraction #5: Screens

I don't love my phone. Instagram is not the most important thing in my life. Checking email is not my top priority. And yet, by the way I spend my time, you'd think it was. I pick up my phone to check it over and over and over again throughout each day. Even if it doesn't ring or buzz, if it's anywhere near me, I unconsciously pick it up to look at it. *Oh, nothing new.* I put the phone down. Three minutes later I do it again.

I'm an intelligent person. I love my family. I know what is important to me, and I even understand the addictive nature of technology. Yet I still struggle with this. I bet you do too. In fact, the average American checks their phone once every ten minutes.[12] And we already know we spend over two hours a day scrolling through social media alone.[13] That's not counting the actual time we are on our phones texting, checking email, reading the news, or playing games. That's insane!

We need to understand that there's a game being played, and we're the ones losing. There are multibillion-dollar companies working really hard to prey on the addictive nature of the human psychology. Their goal is to get us to do what they want us to do—whether that's logging in to Facebook or commenting on posts. They want us scrolling and checking and posting and liking. The more they have our attention, the more we are worth to them and the more they can monetize us to advertisers.

As John Mark Comer says, "Reminder: Your phone doesn't actually work for you. You pay for it, yes. But it works for a multibillion-dollar corporation in California, not for you. You're not the customer; you're the product. It's your attention that's for sale, along with your peace of mind."[14]

The fascinating Netflix docudrama *The Social Dilemma* highlights not only the addictive nature of technology but the brilliant minds and billions of dollars working behind the scenes to distract us from our lives. That may sound dramatic, but there is a reason you check your phone as much as you do and feel you have no control of the compulsion. Large corporations have carefully worked to make this happen.

In the Netflix film, Justin Rosenstein, founder of the Facebook Like button and former Google project manager says, "We are more profitable to a corporation if we're staring at a screen, staring at an ad, than if we are spending that time living our lives in a rich way. And so, we're seeing the results of that. We're seeing corporations using artificial intelligence to outsmart us and figure out how to pull our attention towards the things *they* want us to look at, rather than things that are most consistent with our goals and our values and our lives."[15]

If we're going to have a device in our pocket screaming for our attention all day every day, we are going to need a defense plan. We need to guard ourselves against being sucked into the black hole of technology. We will work on setting boundaries around screens later in the book, but for now, we need to call screens for what they are: distractions. When we start to cut back on the amount of time we spend staring at a screen, we'll be amazed at how much time we have for the things we love and enjoy happening right in front of us. And those are the things that actually make us feel balanced.

> If we're going to have a device in our pocket screaming for our attention all day every day, we are going to need a defense plan.

IDENTIFYING YOUR DISTRACTIONS

In this chapter, we've covered five common distractions—things that most people say aren't important and yet they lose time to. But this list isn't comprehensive because it's not specifically yours. What would you add? What distractions do you get sucked into? Do you find yourself losing time to things you don't care about? Maybe you get distracted by the constant onslaught of news, celebrity gossip, or TV. Or maybe you get distracted by saying yes to every activity or event that you can—but maybe shouldn't—attend. What types of things keep you from focusing on what matters most to you? You get to decide what these things are.

I am not going to tell you what should be important to you and what shouldn't. This is your life, so only you can decide what your distractions are. But if you are having trouble distinguishing between a distraction and what really matters, the list below might help. Something might be a distraction if

- it drains your energy easily
- it stresses you out
- you dread it
- you are doing it out of guilt or obligation
- you don't know why you're doing it

- it makes you feel out of balance
- it makes you become someone you don't like
- it's not very important to you

While we all have things we don't want to do (like change diapers and do taxes), our lives are more in our control than we are often willing to admit. In Step 1 on The Path to Balance, you decided what matters most to you. In Step 2, I want you to decide what doesn't matter so you can stop doing it. Of all the things that you are doing, what can you get rid of? Look back at the five distractions and make a list of where you are losing your time and energy. Maybe yours are the same as those I've included in this chapter, and maybe you have some additional ones. If something isn't very important to you (and you don't have to do it—I mean *really* don't have to do it), it shouldn't get your time. When we create a calendar in the next chapter, these are the things that aren't going to make the cut.

YOU HAVE THE TIME

There's a classic scene from *Saved by the Bell* that my friends and I would quote all the time growing up. To be honest, we still do! Jessie Spano is freaking out to her friend Zack Morris and screams, "No time! There's never any time! I don't have time to study! I'll never get into Stanford!" We always get a good laugh when Jessie's quote fits something that is going on in one of our lives.

But Jessie's words actually ring true for so many of us, and I hear it all the time. "I don't have time to work out! I don't have time to go on a date with my husband! I don't have time to read my Bible!" We say things like this often. The truth is that we have 168 hours in a week. If we sleep seven hours a night and work forty hours a week, we still have roughly seventy-nine hours left to do other things. Seventy-nine hours. We're spending those hours doing *something*.

The same people who tell me they don't have time to work out or go on a date or read their Bible or do any other thing that is important to them are often the same people who know the latest celebrity gossip or know who didn't get a rose on *The Bachelorette*. Now, I don't hate television. I enjoy watching certain shows. But if you know everything about every man on *The Bachelorette* but you don't know about the man living in your own house, you don't have a time problem; you have a priority problem. You have time; you're just spending it on the wrong things.

> **You don't have a time problem; you have a priority problem.**

My friend Curt says, "Distraction is confusion about what's important." I don't want you to be confused about what's important to you. I want you to decide what matters and cut out what doesn't. Because when you get rid of the distractions in your schedule, you not only free yourself up to have more time for things that are actually important to you, but you enjoy them more.

It's how I feel after purging my closet. What's left afterward are items I actually like and wear. I don't have to dig through stuff to find what I want because the only things left are things I want—every option is a good one! When you purge the things that don't matter to you, you feel the same way. The only things left are things that help you be the person you want to be and create the life you want to lead. When you stop doing what doesn't matter to you, you're finally free to become a more balanced you.

JOURNAL QUESTIONS FOR REFLECTION

1. How do you feel when you spend time on things that aren't important to you?
2. What do you think about the idea of "purging" your schedule to create time for what matters most to you?
3. Is it hard to discern what is important or unimportant to you? Why or why not?

Challenge: Your challenge for chapter 4 is to decide what doesn't matter. Use the worksheet for chapter 4: *Decide What Doesn't Matter* in your digital workbook at ramseysolutions.com/tbyt to write a list of things you might want to cut out. In the next chapter, you'll have an opportunity to actually get rid of them!

CHAPTER 5

STEP 3:
CREATE A SCHEDULE THAT REFLECTS WHAT MATTERS

I remember the first magic show I ever saw. I was in the second grade and on a cruise with my dad. As we sat watching the magician perform, I was filled with awe and wonder at his every trick. *He really could cut a woman in half and put her back together! He really could disappear and reappear! He really could hypnotize an entire row of people!*

Magic tricks are fascinating and entertaining to watch, even when you're an adult. Whether the magician accurately guesses your card in the deck or pulls a rabbit out of his hat, it's an amazing experience. But the moment you learn how the magician performs the trick, the mystery and wonder disappear and you realize the tricks aren't that amazing at all. In fact, you see that with some practice, *anyone* could do these tricks.

Creating balance is kind of like that. There are successful men and women everywhere living their version of balance. They are happy and fulfilled, and they are spending their one life on what matters most to them. From a distance, it might look like there's something special about them, like they are the only ones who understand the secret to balance. But the truth is, once you learn their "tricks" for creating balance, you realize that you

> **The third step on The Path to Balance is to create a schedule that reflects what matters.**

can do it too. That's what we are going to dive into in this chapter. The third step on The Path to Balance is to create a schedule that reflects what matters.

CREATING AN IDEAL SCHEDULE

This is where things start to get tactical and you begin to put your priorities into practice. It's time to create a calendar that reflects what matters most to you. Your calendar is your life. Your calendar reflects how you use your minutes and hours and days and years. It reflects the life you are going to lead, so let's make sure it matches the one that you want.

But before we get started, I want you to gather four things you will need. If you downloaded your Take Back Your Time Workbook, all of these things except your current schedule will be included in that. If you haven't, you can download that at ramseysolutions.com/tbyt to use it for this step.

1. **Your What Matters Most List.** This is the list you created in Step 1 (chapter 3). Keep this list nearby as you create your ideal calendar. These are the things you decided were important, so your calendar should reflect those things.

2. **Your list of priorities for this season.** You also created this list in Step 1. It will help you create a calendar that is current for what is happening in this season and relevant to what is most important to you right now.

3. **A current weekly calendar.** This is the schedule that you are working with and living in. It may be a physical calendar on your kitchen wall or your planner, or it may live within the calendar app on your phone. It will probably include tasks or events for work, school, family, or church.

4. **A blank copy of a weekly calendar.** This is included in your Take Back Your Time Workbook. You can also open up a weekly calendar on your computer or turn to a blank week in your planner.

Now that you have these four things, we are going to use them to create a new weekly schedule that reflects your version of balance and what matters most to you. We will call this your ideal schedule. Here's how the process works: I will walk you through several stages to create this. At each stage, you're going to look at your current schedule and move things over to your new ideal schedule. Some things will get carried over as we walk through this and some won't. You will also have an opportunity to add new things. Once you are finished, this will be your ideal schedule. Although we say "ideal," we understand that each week will look slightly different as your weekly priorities shift and change. This is simply a guide to get you started.

Things You Have to Do

To start, look at your current schedule and move over everything you know you absolutely must do to the blank weekly calendar. These are the things in your life that you cannot move or that you don't want to move. For example, you probably want to sleep at night when the rest of the world is sleeping, so you will block those nighttime hours for sleep. You may have a full-time job that you work from 8:00–5:00. If so, block those hours. For this first step, you just want to carry over current commitments that you absolutely *must* do. Very few things probably fall into this category.

I want to point out one important thing here, though. If while doing this, you realize you're adding something to your ideal calendar that you really don't want to do, that stresses you out, or that you dread doing every single day, it's a very strong clue that something needs to change. You'll never feel balanced if you hate how you spend a large portion of your time.

For example, say that you're a night nurse and you hate the hours because you never see your family. You may not be able to move to the day shift this week or even this month, but it doesn't mean you have to accept being miserable for the rest of your career. Even though you may not be able to fix this right now, you can make a note to yourself to work on changing it. We will talk more about how to do that below.

Things You Want to Do

After you fill in the things you have to do, such as sleep and work, now it's time to start adding the things you want to do. For this, you're going to need your What Matters Most List and seasonal priorities from Step 1. First, read your lists and, with those things in mind, look at your current calendar. What commitments from your current calendar do you want to move to your new one? What activities and responsibilities excite you and make you light up and come alive? Which ones reflect what matters most to you and enable you to be the person you want to be? Which things are important to you in this season? Move each of those things to your ideal schedule.

For example, I tend to feel like the state of my house. If my house looks good, I feel good. If my house is a wreck, I feel like a wreck! It's hard for me to feel balanced in a messy house, so I try to make cleaning a priority for that reason. I don't *want* to clean but having a somewhat clean house is important to me, so that makes it on my calendar. I've also noticed that if I can't get outside and move my body week after week, or if I don't spend time with God in some way each week, I get grouchy. I need to be outside and spend time with God to feel like myself, so I plan time each week to do those things. What about you? What are the things that make you feel balanced and more like who you want to be?

Once you add those things, then you'll start to plug in *new* things that you want to do—things that maybe you've never had time for. Maybe you've always wanted to take an online class or tennis lessons, but you've never been able to fit it in. Or maybe you want alone time each morning before you start your day. Look at your ideal schedule and block time for those things.

Now, take one more look at your What Matters Most List. What is missing from your calendar that reflects what matters most to you right now? What is missing that will help you feel balanced? If spending time with family is something that matters most, does your weekly schedule reflect that? If volunteering matters most to you, is that represented in your schedule? If you want to reach a new goal, like run a 5K or start a side business in this season, are those things reflected anywhere on your calendar? Take some time now to add things to your new schedule that reflect what's important to you.

What you have created is your ideal schedule. You and I both know there is hardly ever a perfect week, but this gives you something to start from and build on as your priorities change. As you update your schedule each week to reflect your current weekly and daily priorities, you can use this as a template to work from. The more you can align your life with your priorities—the right things—the more balanced you will feel. Remember, life balance isn't about doing everything for an equal amount of time. It's about doing the right things at the right time. It's about spending your life on what matters to you. So if something matters, it needs to make it on the calendar or it won't happen.

> **If something matters, it needs to make it on the calendar or it won't happen.**

Things That Don't Make the Cut

When you sit back and look at your new schedule next to your current one, you'll probably notice some differences. More than likely, there are things on your current calendar that didn't get moved over to your ideal one. Do you know why? Because you don't *have* to do them or you don't *want* to do them—or both! That means they are not a priority right now and they should not get your time.

Keep in mind, just because something isn't right *right now*, doesn't mean it never will be. For example, I'd like to do a ton of things—like play soccer in an adult league again or travel overseas. I will do those things one day, but none of them is right for me right now. None of them is a priority in this season of life. And because they aren't right for me right now, if I tried to squeeze them into my schedule anyway, they would stress me out tremendously. Not right now doesn't mean never. It just means not right now.

You get to choose what makes it to your new calendar and what doesn't, what you're fighting for and what you are willing to let go of. I love how my friend Rory Vaden says, "Anything on your calendar is either something you put there or something you allowed to be there." The more you fill your time and your life with things that really matter the most to you right now, the more balanced you will feel. So don't feel guilty for cutting things that don't matter to you or for cutting things that aren't right in this season.

Remember, no one gets to tell you what should be important to you.

Whether you have your wedding in a church or outside, or you spend your time on this thing or that, you are the only one who gets to decide what's important to you. And you don't have to figure it all out on your own. If you take the time to pause and pray, God can and will show you your deepest desires and what's important to you. He will lead you toward his plans for you. And then, what matters the most is that you spend your life on what matters most to you.

> **What matters the most is that you spend your life on what matters most to you.**

A RECIPE FOR BALANCE

I love making chicken salad, and I have about twenty-seven different ways I enjoy making it. Some with pecans and some with almonds. Some with green onions and some with red. Some with grapes and some with apples. Regardless of which combination I choose, there are a few things that I add to almost every batch. Those ingredients are chicken (obviously), some type of nut, some type of sauce, some type of fruit, some type of onion, and celery. If you don't have most of those things, it's probably not going to taste like chicken salad.

Balance has some necessary ingredients too. There are five things that are just nonnegotiable if you want to feel balanced. These are rest, relationships, help, work you enjoy, and time alone. Let's take a look at each of these.

1. Rest

The adult human body needs seven to eight hours of sleep per night to function, but most people aren't getting that. When we try to get more done, often the first thing to drop off our priority list is sleep. And we're struggling because of it.

Research shows that when we don't get enough sleep, we experience a lack of alertness, impaired memory, relationship stress, a reduced quality of life, and even an increased likelihood of a car accident. If you continue to operate without enough sleep for a prolonged period of time, this can lead to even more serious and long-term health problems like high blood pressure, diabetes, heart attack or heart failure, and stroke.[16]

When we don't get enough sleep or we don't sleep well, we are cranky, unproductive, and out of sorts. If you're going to have any sense of balance in your life, you have to stop skipping sleep and start incorporating this into your life like it actually matters. Because it does.

2. Relationships

I believe God created us to be in relationship with one another. We all felt this in a very real way during the 2020 pandemic, especially people who lived alone. We weren't created to live isolated from each other. Even if you're an introvert and enjoy your time alone, you still need connection, whether those relationships are with family, friends, coworkers, church family, or people in your community.

Tony Robbins says, "The quality of your life is the quality of your relationships." In fact, studies show that strong social connections improve the quality of your life, and they also have a direct correlation with reduced health issues, less depression, and a longer life span. One study even found that people with strong social connections were less likely to develop a cold after exposure to a virus![17] But you don't need research to tell you something you already know: relationships matter. If you want to have balance, you have to be intentional about connecting with others.

3. Help

If you're going to create balance in your life, you're going to need help doing it. Having people in your corner to help you is important for you to do the things you want to do and actually enjoy your life. (And by the way, the help you give others allows them to do the same!) No one can do everything on their own.

Whether it's family helping with childcare or team members helping with work projects, you need help if you want to feel balanced. For example, I'm so grateful for my husband, Matt, my mom who lives three miles down the road, my dad and stepmom, and my in-laws. I'm also thankful for our incredible nanny who has been a part of our family for the past four years. We're a team, and we all love each other and help each other in different ways.

If you don't have family nearby or don't have the budget for childcare, there are still creative ways to get help. For example, two of my friends swap babysitting nights for each other so the other couple can have a date night. Churches often host "parents night out" events so parents can go out or have some "time off." And many ministries provide help for those who need car maintenance or home repairs. Look to your friends, family, or community for resources, and don't be too proud to ask for help.

4. Work You Enjoy

Did you know that, according to research, 85 percent of employees worldwide aren't engaged in their jobs?[18] That's crazy! You spend too much time doing what you do to be miserable doing it. And if you are giving up over forty of your waking hours to something you dread, you will never feel balanced. Whether you work inside or outside the home, you need to spend your time doing something you love.

If you are doing something for a season just to get by, that's one thing . . . and we will talk more about that in chapter 8. But if you have resigned yourself to the lie that this has to be your life, I have news for you: it doesn't. This does not have to be your life. You do not have to spend your one life doing something you hate. You can find a way to make money doing what you love, whether that's by starting your own business—which is what I love helping people do through my book *Business Boutique* and our Business Boutique events—or by finding your dream job, which is what my friend Ken Coleman loves helping people do on *The Ken Coleman Show* and in his books *The Proximity Principle* and *From Paycheck to Purpose*.

I'm not saying you need to have a Jerry Maguire moment where you grab the goldfish and walk out on your steady paycheck tomorrow. I am saying that you need to start working on a plan to do something different. You will never feel balanced if you hate how you spend your days. You need to do some type of work that you enjoy, at least most of the time, if you want to have any sense of balance.

5. Time Alone

According to Amy Morin, author of *13 Things Mentally Strong People Don't Do*, the busier you are, the more likely you are to benefit from alone time. She says there are actually science-based reasons for spending time alone: Alone time increases empathy and productivity. It sparks creativity. It builds mental strength. And it helps you know yourself.[19] It is critical to our overall health and well-being.

> **You will never feel balanced if you hate how you spend your days.**

My friend Sarah never had time alone. As an extrovert who loved people, she didn't realize just how much she needed alone time until she didn't have it anymore. And since she was a single mom doing everything on her own, it was that much harder to get any time for herself. Every waking minute, she was either at work with other people or at home with her daughter. And to make a hard situation even more difficult, her daughter wasn't sleeping well at the time.

After years of no sleep and never having a moment alone, Sarah finally decided something needed to change. She started using drop-in daycares and asking friends for help. At first she fought the guilt of leaving her daughter with others so she could have some time for herself, but she quickly realized how vital alone time was for her own health.

If you are around people all day every day, whether at work or home or both, you need to create time to be alone. Maybe that means waking up before everyone in the house to have fifteen minutes to yourself. Maybe it means going for a short walk by yourself when everyone else is occupied in the evenings. If you want to maintain your balance, and your sanity, you've got to have some time alone.

As you create your own recipe for balance, throwing in a dash of this or a pinch of that, make sure it includes these five ingredients. They are critical for your physical and emotional health, and they will help you maintain a sense of balance in your life.

WHAT NEEDS TO CHANGE?

After creating your ideal weekly schedule, you might start to see some problems. You might realize that you never get enough sleep or you have commitments that you need to get rid of. You might realize that you spend a lot of time on something you hate (like in a job in a toxic work culture). When this happens, I encourage you to make a note for yourself. There is an exercise to help you do this in your Take Back Your Time Workbook at ramseysolutions.com/tbyt, where you can capture things you want to change and then create a plan to fix it. In the example of the night nurse who wants to spend more time with her family, she might capture this goal and then, over the next three months, work to fix this part of her schedule. For someone else who has committed to volunteer in something they don't actually want to do (like coaching a soccer team!), they can create a plan to try to find somebody who might be willing to take over or fill in for them over time.

I don't want you to immediately walk out of every commitment that your heart isn't into anymore. Burning bridges and letting people down isn't a way to create balance. But I do want you to recognize things that need to change in your life that are keeping you from the life you want to lead. You might not be working your ideal schedule by next week, but with some intentionality and effort, you can likely get there over the next few months.

From Ideal Schedule to Actual Schedule

You've created an ideal schedule that reflects what matters most to you right now, but this schedule is simply a guide to get you started. It most likely doesn't accurately reflect your actual schedule right now. While you can't snap your fingers and work your ideal schedule overnight, you can begin to work toward it. A good rule of thumb I use when coaching people in time management is the 25/4 rule: change your current schedule by 25 percent each week over the next four weeks.

Maybe week 1 you sign up for that class you've been wanting to take and set an earlier bedtime. Then by week 2, you've found help with childcare so you can have that weekly date night with your spouse. By week 3 you might have found someone else to coach the soccer team so you can remove that commitment from your schedule, and then by week 4, you're able to fix your work hours that were stressing you out. If you make about 25 percent of the changes you want each week for four weeks, you should be living in your ideal schedule in about a month. Of course this is not a perfect formula, but it does give you something to work toward and a way to work toward it.

Weekly Rhythms

Even after you are working in your ideal schedule, you'll still need to have a way of managing your time and commitments each week. Whether you use a paper planner like my Goal Planner or an app on your phone or something else, you'll still need to update your schedule each week to reflect the commitments you have going on at that time. That's why I want you to get into a weekly rhythm of revisiting your schedule. Here's what this looks like in a practical way:

- Pick a day of the week when you will plan for the following week.
- Set your priorities for that next week.
- Connect with your family on everyone's plans.
- Write down the schedule somewhere visible for everyone to see (in addition to the calendar you use for yourself).

I do this each week on Sunday night. Every Sunday night, I look at the week ahead. I establish my priorities for that particular week, and I have a conversation with my husband about his plans and anything out of the ordinary going on. That might look like:

"I have a late meeting on Tuesday. Can you take Carter to basketball practice that afternoon? We have a parent-teacher meeting Thursday at 10:00. Can you go with me to that? Are you out of town on Friday for work? If so, I'll take the kids to visit my dad while you're gone."

Once we sync up on the schedule, I fill in the wet-erase weekly calendar on our refrigerator so everyone can see what's going on. This simple system becomes a weekly rhythm that not only allows me to be on the same page with my family, but that also helps me keep my priorities front and center so I'm spending my time on what matters most. It also gives me permission to be flexible. I understand that no two weeks are ever the same, and as my priorities change, my schedule will too.

Daily Rhythms and To-Do Lists

As we think about our weekly rhythm of creating calendars and schedules, we also need to think about our to-do lists and how they affect our daily routines. Most of us have these lists, whether they live in our heads (*the three things I must get done today are . . .*) or on our phones or on an organized paper calendar. To-do lists are tied to our schedules and our days, so we have to learn how to create them and use them in a way that helps us without sucking us into the addictive cycle of empty busyness. We can do that with a simple system to help us.

Charles M. Schwab was the president of the Bethlehem Steel Corporation about a hundred years ago. His company was having a hard time with productivity, so Schwab brought in a man named Ivy Lee. Lee was a popular efficiency expert, and he agreed to help, saying to Schwab, "After three months, you can send me a check for whatever you feel it's worth to you."

After spending time interviewing many of the leaders in the company, Lee's suggestion was simple. He told the management team to write a to-do list at the end of each day and include the top six tasks they needed to get done the following day, in order of priority. They followed his advice, and the team began following their to-do lists from top to bottom every day. Apparently, after the three months, the company was so much more efficient that Schwab sent a check to Lee for $25,000—the equivalent of more than $400,000 today![20] This example—now called the Ivy Lee Method—shows the power of the to-do list.

Like we talked about before, the to-do list can be both a good thing and a bad thing, depending on how we use it.

It can help us stay focused and be more productive, as the example above shows. It can also become an addictive cycle of productivity where we chase checked boxes. We obsessively fill it up with things—many of which aren't even important—and then we beat ourselves up when we don't get them done. In fact, a recent survey of 2,000 adults found that the average person has fourteen undone items on their to-do lists, and 59 percent of the participants said keeping their lives organized with everything they have going on was a "big struggle."[21]

> I don't want to help you just get *more* things done, I want to help you get the right things done—the things that create balance in your life.

So how do we do it? How can we use a to-do list to help us stay organized and not let it ruin our lives? I don't want to help you just get *more* things done, I want to help you get the right things done—the things that create balance in your life. The to-do list can be a valuable tool, but if it's going to help us, we need to understand how to use it in the right way and how it connects to the calendar we just created.

What You Want to Get Done Most Today

Like we talked about in chapter 3, you want to begin each day by deciding what your priorities are for that day. This will be your to-do list for the day. These are the things you want to get done the most. In fact, I encourage you to title your list exactly that: "What I Want to Get Done Most Today." As silly as it may sound, when you go to fill in this list, the title will help you remember that this list should only include things you really want to get done the most. If you get nothing else done, these are the things you want to get done the *most*. Write your list of what those three to five priorities are at the beginning of each day. Once you write those down, look at your schedule for the day and decide where to fit them in to make sure they can actually happen. Deciding what is most important at the beginning of each day will help you adapt your plans as things change throughout the week, and it will help you continue to do the right things at the right time.

I can't tell you how many times I've planned at the beginning of the week what I'm going to do every day, but as the week goes on, things change. Things come up, my plans get derailed, and my energy usually declines. Then when I can't complete the to-do list I planned at the beginning of the week—when I was so energetic and optimistic—of course I feel guilty. Setting priorities at the beginning of each day helps put a stop to that exhausting cycle. This daily habit helps you focus on one day at a time, which reduces overwhelm. It also helps you make decisions based on what is going on and how you're feeling each individual day.

But you and I both know there are several other things you might like to do if you could get around to them. Right now, you might be mixing those less important things in with the real priorities on your to-do list. You have "pick up prescription" right next to "reorganize the attic." Every time you look at this long, cluttered list, your brain is working extra hard to discern what you *really* want to get done most *today* from all the random ideas you *might* want to do *sometime*. But like me, you probably want to capture those ideas just in case you do have some extra time and want to tackle them. That's why I keep a separate list to organize these tasks and ideas, and you can too.

Other Things You Could Do If You Have Time

In addition to my "What I Want to Get Done Most" list of priorities, I have a separate list titled "Other Things I Could Do If I Have Time." By titling this list this way, my brain is able to relax. I'm reminded that I don't *have* to do these tasks. I *could* do them if I decide to. There's no pressure to complete them and no guilt if they don't get done. These tasks are not urgent or important. They are just random ideas that pop into my head. This list is extremely helpful because it becomes a catch-all for every idea—from cleaning up the playroom to tweezing your eyebrows to powerwashing the deck—without cluttering up your actual list of priorities that you really need and want to get done on any given day. By having two separate lists, you can easily see what is an actual priority and what's just a nice idea that you might want to get around to if there's time left over.

This system becomes a very simple way to prioritize tasks based on importance and when they need to get done. It helps you see what actually matters today without being distracted by random ideas you wrote down on a whim. This system also gives you permission to ignore all the tasks that are not urgent or important. If you happen to have some free time open up and you want to pick something on your "Other Things I Could Do If I Have Time" list, you can. But this process will save you from feeling guilty every time you check your to-do list and see "clean baseboards" or "purge kids' toys" staring at you like they have been the past three weeks. What you actually need to get done today will be clear.

We live by our calendars and to-do lists. And we'll never feel balanced if we spend our time and energy showing up to commitments we don't care about and checking off boxes on lists that don't really even matter. That's why we have to put our priorities on paper on purpose. When we begin to align our calendars and to-do lists with what actually matters, we will not only get the right things done, but we'll actually have more fun and feel more balanced as well.

SYSTEMS FOR SUCCESS

Pastor Craig Groeschel spoke once at one of our EntreLeadership events on something that, at first glance, seemed incredibly boring—systems. That doesn't sound exciting at all, right? I didn't think so either when he started speaking. But then he unpacked what systems do for us in business and in life, and it was like someone turned on a light in a dark room for me. Being a free-spirited person, I've always felt a little bogged down by rules and processes. But as he explained that day, we all have systems. We either have them by intent or by default. He said, "They are a result of what you've created or what you've tolerated." Dang. That's good.

I realized that I already had systems for things in my life; they just weren't good ones. I had a system of setting an alarm each night . . . that I would respond to by hitting snooze sixty-seven times each morning. I had a system of making lunches each morning before school, which made me feel rushed before leaving the house. I had a system of panic-buying outfits for my work events at the last minute, which stressed me out. I had systems for a lot of things, but my systems were terrible. Pastor Groeschel taught me that by changing my systems, I could change my outcome. "Goals don't determine success," he said. "Systems do." I had honestly never thought about systems that way, but it opened my eyes to something I not only knew I needed but that I wanted.

And you know what? Calendars and to-do lists are just systems. They are systems for setting your priorities, managing your time, and controlling your life. That's all they are. They are tools that help you be the person you want to be, do the things you want to do, and live the life you want to lead. Systems might not seem exciting, but if they help make those things possible, then that *is* exciting! If you want to create your own version of balance, you need to create a calendar—a helpful system—that reflects what matters to you and makes that balance possible.

JOURNAL QUESTIONS FOR REFLECTION

1. Is keeping a schedule or calendar hard or easy for you?
2. Was it hard to not move certain things over to your new, ideal schedule?
3. How do you feel about the new, ideal calendar you created?

Challenge: Your challenge for chapter 5 is to create a schedule that reflects what matters. Use the worksheet for chapter 5: *Create a Schedule that Reflects What Matters* in your digital workbook at ramseysolutions.com/tbyt to work through each of the exercises in this chapter. Ask your family to do this calendar exercise with you. Each of you can share how you want to use your time and what you want to work toward, both individually and as a family.

CHAPTER 6

STEP 4:
PROTECT WHAT MATTERS

S usan really needed to give more. She needed to give more time and more money. At least that's what the leaders of the organization she was a volunteer member of thought. And Susan heard about it regularly. She needed to host events, volunteer often, and of course, donate. She needed to be at every meeting and on every call and *yes, it was very important* and *no, she really could not miss it*. It didn't matter how much Susan did, how much she showed up, or how much she gave of her time, money, and energy. It wasn't enough.

Even though the commitment had become overwhelming, Susan loved this organization. She had been a part of it for over a decade and held a leadership position there. Not only that, she had made some of her best friends in her new city through this close-knit community. But Susan was starting to realize that her heart wasn't in it anymore, and the commitment was more than she was up for at this point in her life. She also realized that the reason she initially wanted to volunteer with and support this organization was no longer why she was there. She spent her time and energy worrying if she was pleasing the people in the group who kept trying to push her around. Something had to change. It was time to start saying no, and it was time to cut ties.

But how would she do it? How could she walk away from women she had become so close with? Their calendars were so intertwined that if Susan left, she wouldn't just be breaking up with the organization but with the people in it, depending on how they took the news. She'd also be sending a shockwave through her schedule. The whole process of leaving and then communicating it to everyone was stressful. She did it, but not without some heartache.

The fourth step on The Path to Balance is to protect what matters.

Susan is one of the most confident, go-getter women I know. Still, she struggled with protecting her time, saying no, and stepping back. We've all been there. Even if you know making a decision is right, it doesn't mean it's easy. But the reality is that unless we learn how to protect what matters to us, our entire lives will be dictated by other people who feel it's their duty to tell us what to do. This is *your* life. You have to protect your time so that you can spend it on what's important to *you*.

PROTECTING WHAT'S IMPORTANT TO YOU

For most people, saying no and standing their ground is incredibly hard. We all want to be liked and we all want to help. We don't want to come across as rude or selfish. But the good news is, we don't have to. We can be kind and loving while still being honest and firm. Protecting your schedule doesn't make you a bad person. It makes you a wise one.

If you don't protect what's important to you, you can guarantee that you're going to be pushed around. You will agree to commitments that you end up resenting and regretting later. You'll give up your money, time, and peace of mind. You'll say yes when you want to say no. You'll buy the magazines from the salesman at the door because *well, he just seemed so sweet.* You'll agree to be the homeroom mom for your child's class because *well, they did ask me specifically to do it.* You'll volunteer to coach your son's soccer team because *well, they didn't have anyone else.* You'll do things you don't want to do with time you don't have to please people you don't owe anything to. You'll become bitter and burnt out, unhappy and overwhelmed. You'll become a person you don't like in a life you don't like. And you'll be right back out of balance.

That's why the fourth step on The Path to Balance is to protect what matters. Even after you create a schedule that reflects what matters to you, you still have to protect it by setting boundaries and saying no. And you know what? You're going to need confidence to do that.

WHERE CONFIDENCE COMES FROM

If you want to protect your schedule, you're going to need confidence to guard against pushy people. If you want the gusto to say no, you're going to need confidence to do so. If you want to set boundaries with others, you'll need confidence to stand your ground. If you're going to fight the temptation to be the hero, you're going to need confidence. But where does confidence come from? I believe true confidence comes from three main places: faith, courage, and practice. Let's look at each of those.

Having Faith Gives You Confidence

There's an inner peace that comes from knowing who you are and whose you are. When you rest in the truth of what God says about you in his Word—like that you are created, chosen, loved, and accepted, to name just a few examples—you become comfortable in your own skin and okay with being you. You don't have to strive to earn everyone's approval, and you don't have to tiptoe around everyone's opinions of you. Author and speaker Annie F. Downs says, "The more I know God, the more sure I am of me." I love that! When you rest in the truth of who you are and whose you are according to God's Word, it gives you peace, grace, and, most of all, confidence.

Faith can also put life into perspective. When we're facing something difficult or challenging and our natural inclination is to swoop in and fix the problem ourselves, we're reminded: that's God's role, not ours. That's an important reminder when we are fighting the urge to save the day. Because believe it or not, the world will go on just fine without our help. We can and should help where we feel led and called, but that's very different from feeling guilty and obligated. The weight of the world was never meant to be on our shoulders.

Faith also builds confidence when you remember that God is completely and always in control. No matter what happens on this earth, God isn't up in heaven pacing around and wringing his hands, saying, "How in the world did I miss this?! I never saw it coming!" That just doesn't happen.

I can't tell you how many times life has thrown me a curveball that sent me reeling. In those moments when I find myself freaking out, I stop and remind myself that God is never surprised. Never. He knew this was going to happen and he is still on his throne. His Word even tells us to be confident. Hebrews 10:35 says, "Do not throw away your confidence; it will be richly rewarded." And Hebrews 11:1 says, "Now *faith is confidence* in what we hope for and assurance about what we do not see" (emphasis added). God wants us to have confidence, and when we are rooted in him, we will find the confidence we need.

When you and I remember these things, we have all the reason in the world for complete confidence. We realize in good times and in hard times that our confidence isn't in ourselves and our ability anyway. Our confidence is in the God of the universe who put every star in the sky and every hair on your head and every dream in your heart. He knows everything, he can do anything, and he's always on time. We can remember that no matter what happens, God's got this, and most of all, he's got us. That's a foundation of confidence that can't be taken away.

Being Courageous Creates Confidence

Even if your faith is strong and you know that God is for you, it doesn't mean you will always *feel* confident. This is where courage comes in. For example, when I walked onstage for my very first speaking event, I was scared out of my mind. My legs were shaking, my palms were sweating, and my heart was racing. I was a nervous wreck! I knew God was in control, but I had no idea what I was doing. I also had no idea how the audience would respond. The entire event felt like a slow-motion scene from a movie. For the first time in my life, I heard my own voice boom through giant speakers to more than 1,000 teenagers (talk about a tough first crowd!). I forced a smile and said, with every ounce of feigned enthusiasm I could muster: "Hey, y'all! I'm so excited to be here!"

Boldface. Lie. I was not excited to be there. I was freaking terrified to be there! I was shaking and sweating and trying not to hyperventilate. But I didn't walk out there and show that. I didn't put my hands in my pockets and mumble into the microphone, "Hey, y'all. I'm really nervous . . . I don't know what I'm doing." That would have been a disaster in every possible way. It would have done a disservice to the crowd and only reinforced the fear I was already feeling.

So I was courageous and just faked it. I faked feeling confident at that first speaking event and several after that. I've faked it every time I stand on a stage in front of a larger crowd than I've ever spoken to before. I just throw my shoulders back, force a smile, and say that I'm excited to be there. You can act courageous and fake it until you feel it.

And you know what? After a decade of doing that, I actually mean it now. I feel confident walking onstage, and I am genuinely excited to be there. But that didn't happen because I was born with some special "ability-to-speak-in-front-of-large-crowds" gene. It happened because I was courageous and I faked it. I faked feeling confident until I actually felt confident.

According to research, it's actually a good strategy. It even has a name: "status-enhancement theory." The way the theory works is that "people gain influence by acting dominant and confident. Doing so gives others the impression that you're a competent person."[22] Then, when you actually pull that thing off with competence, guess what? You gain confidence!

You can act courageous and fake it until you feel it.

So just like I faked it until I felt it, you can too. When you put yourself out there and do something you're scared to do and you survive (because I promise you will), your confidence grows. But just doing it one time isn't enough. You have to keep doing it over and over and over. This is where practice comes in.

Practicing Builds Confidence

When I joined the track team in high school, I expected to run every day like we did in middle school. I was surprised that a couple of times a week, our coach had us in the weight room lifting weights. Weights? For female high school runners? I had never done strength training before, so this made no sense to me. I followed the coach's instructions, but I didn't feel like these workouts had much purpose when we were trying to get faster, not build muscle. After a few weeks, I noticed that my event times were getting faster and faster. My coach explained that the weightlifting had been making my muscles stronger. When my muscles were stronger, they could do more. They could propel me faster around the track.

Confidence is like a muscle. While some personality styles tend to be more fearless, confidence is a skill that anyone can learn and a muscle that anyone can strengthen. If you rarely show confidence, then you just need to strengthen that muscle through exercise and practice. You are going to feel weak and even a little wobbly at first. That's normal. But like with weight-lifting, the more you exercise a muscle, the stronger it will become. The stronger it becomes, the more you can do with it.

Just like public speaking got a little easier every time for me, things requiring confidence will become easier for you.

Over time and through practice, you'll build genuine, authentic, unshakable confidence. But it doesn't happen overnight. It happens by practicing over time.

With some practice, you will realize that you *can* have the confidence to protect your time. You *can* have the confidence to stop doing the wrong things and start doing the right things. You *can* feel more powerful, like you actually have a say in your own life. Imagine that!

HOW TO PROTECT WHAT MATTERS TO YOU

In the previous chapter, you created a schedule that *reflected* what matters most to you. Now you are going to learn to *protect* what matters most to you. You are going to learn to lean on your confidence to practice protecting your calendar and your life. The two main ways you do this are by setting boundaries and saying no.

Setting Boundaries

Annie F. Downs takes every Wednesday as a sabbath. On that day, she doesn't use social media or do any work at all. She doesn't have any commitments. She just rests. That sounds amazing, doesn't it? You might think that Annie has all the time in the world. If so, you'd be wrong. Annie is busier than most people I know and juggles an overwhelming amount of responsibilities. She doesn't *have* time for a day of rest; she *makes* time for it.

What does that mean? For Annie, Wednesdays are protected. So if someone asks her to do something on a Wednesday, she already knows the answer. She doesn't have to think about it. She has decided in advance how she's going to spend her Wednesdays, and the boundary does the work for her.

Just like Annie sets boundaries and protects them, you can do this in your own life. Maybe you want to set a boundary that no one uses their phones between 5:00 and 7:00 p.m. during dinner and family time, like our family does. Or you decide you need to set a boundary around your screen time, so you have a thirty-minute time limit each day for social media apps on your phone. Or if date nights are important to you like they are for my friends Tyler and Hanna, you set a boundary that every Thursday night is date night, and unless something super important comes up, it doesn't get bumped. Or if you feel video games are taking over your kids' brains, set a boundary that video games or devices are off-limits on weekdays in your house. The thing is, you get to decide what's right for you and your family.

Boundaries teach people how to respect you, and they hold you accountable to doing what you say you want to do.

Boundaries also take the thinking out of making decisions. And let's be honest, when you're already worn out, that's a great thing! If someone asks you to work late on date night or go to coffee on your workout morning, you don't have to even think about the decision. The boundary has already made the decision for you.

Of course, if something special comes up and you want to "break" your own rule, you can. But that should be the exception. The majority of the time, you have a boundary around things that are important to you to protect you and your time. This is vital because, as we talked about before, if you don't protect what matters to you, no one else will.

Saying No

Jenny is one of my most considerate friends. She never wants to make waves or ruffle feathers. She doesn't like conflict or awkwardness, and she will go to great lengths to avoid it. Once, when we were in our mid-twenties, Jenny and I were at a restaurant with a group of friends. As we were waiting to be seated, a man walked up to her and started chatting. They talked for a while and then he walked away.

The moment he was out of earshot she turned to me and said "*UGH!* I hate that he has my number!" I asked the obvious question: "What? Why did you give it to him?" She said, "Well, he asked . . . I couldn't just say no." I said, "Yes, you can! It's *your* number!"

And you know what? It's also *your* time. You don't only have the right to say no, you have the responsibility to. If someone has the nerve to ask you to do something you don't want to do, you need to have the nerve to say no. Whether it's for your number, for your time, or for your help, you're not obligated just because someone asked.

> **You don't only have the right to say no, you have the responsibility to.**

An honest no is always better than a dishonest yes. And as Anne Lamott has said, "No is a complete sentence." You don't need to apologize for it, justify it, or explain it. Just no. When you tell the truth, it doesn't just benefit you. It also benefits the other person. When you say no to people from time to time, your words actually carry weight. People will respect you more. Then, when you do say yes to something, people will know that you actually want to be there.

Henry Cloud says it so well in his book *Boundaries*: "People . . . who can respect our boundaries will love our wills, our opinions, our separateness. Those who can't . . . are telling us that they don't love our no. They only love our yes, our compliance."[23]

So, if someone asks you to go out on a Friday night but you just want to stay home in your pajamas watching a movie on the couch, guess what? You can say that! You don't have to make up an excuse or say yes only to wriggle out of it at the last minute. Instead, you can have the integrity to be honest about what you're going to do. (Remember, this is *your* life and you don't need to apologize for spending it how *you* want to.) You might say something like, "Thank you so much for inviting me! I'm actually looking forward to a night at home on the couch watching a movie, but I hope you have fun!"

Did you notice there that you can say no without ever even saying the word? My husband does this to me all the time. Let's say that I come home with a new idea to move to a new house. Or get a dog. Or buy a pontoon boat. (Each of those may or may not be real ideas that I have presented to him very enthusiastically in the past few months alone.)

So let's say that I come home with one of these new ideas that I am super passionate about. Matt will usually respond with, "Wow, babe! That's really interesting. I don't think now is the right time to add [insert crazy new idea here] to our busy lives, but we can definitely talk about it in the future." So nice. The answer is still no. You don't have to be a jerk, and

I hope you aren't. But you can be honest and politely decline offers that aren't right for you in a way that's true to your personality and style. When you do, you're not only exercising your confidence muscle, you're also protecting your time and your life.

WHEN YOU DON'T KNOW WHAT TO DO

Should I do this? Yes! No, wait. No, definitely not. Well, maybe . . . I don't know!

I can't tell you how many times I have had an internal debate with myself over whether or not I should do something. Even though I am perfectly capable of saying no, I am not sure when I should. We all want to do the right things, but how are we supposed to know what the right things are? Ironically, this happened to me just this week. Remember when I volunteered to coach my son's soccer team and vowed that, pregnant or not, I would not ever do that again?

Well, since then, Carter has changed his mind and apparently loves soccer again. He's been begging me all year to sign him up to play, so after waiting several months to see if he was serious about it, I finally gave in. I signed him up and began looking forward to relaxing on the sidelines in a camping chair like all the other normal parents.

Then, just this week, I received an email from the organization. They don't have a coach for his team. I know. I couldn't make this up if I tried. After waiting a few days, I received another email—this one even more desperate—begging one of the parents to step up and volunteer to coach the team. Cue internal debate:

No. Just no. You are not doing this.

But they really need someone! What are they going to do?!

Figure something else out, that's what. Not your problem.

What if no one steps up? What if someone does and they are terrible?

Then so be it. You're not doing this. Resist!

But you can totally do this! You've played and coached before! They need you!

What happened to relaxing in a camp chair on the sidelines? Remember that?

You can still have fun while leading the kindergartners through drills.

The answer is no. Stop asking.

Ever been there? I have—this week and anytime an opportunity comes up that I'm not sure how to respond to. You wring your hands and pace around, trying to figure out what to do. You want to protect your schedule, but you aren't sure *when* to. When do you say yes and when do you say no? And what questions should you ask yourself to make the right decision?

Stop Asking the Wrong Questions

Years ago, when I was faced with a decision, I would only ask myself these two questions:

1. Do they need me? *(Yes, of course they do. That's why they're asking.)*
2. Can I do it? *(Let me just find a sliver of time on my calendar to cram this in.)*

That's it. Those were the only questions I asked myself. My guess is, that's what most people do.

Let's go ahead and acknowledge a couple of problems with this decision-making strategy. The first problem is, if these are your only questions, you have no way to say no if you don't have plans. If the time is open and available, you believe you are obligated to say yes. After all, they need you and you have the time. You technically *can* do it. So you say yes every time your calendar is open. The second problem with this decision-making strategy is that when you live your life this way, you will have every spare minute scheduled for someone else. It just depends on who gets to you first or who is the loudest, the neediest, or has the best guilt trip.

This isn't a good way to make decisions or live your life. I want to share some wisdom that my mom shared with me years ago. She said, "Just because you *can* do something does not mean that you *should*. Just because someone *needs* you doesn't *obligate* you." Read that again. Just because someone needs you doesn't obligate you. Your life and your time is just that—*yours*. You must learn to protect your time and start asking better questions before committing to something.

> Just because you *can* do something does not mean that you *should*. Just because someone *needs* you doesn't *obligate* you.

Start Asking the Right Questions

So what is a better decision-making strategy for choosing to say yes or no? Instead of only asking yourself the two questions above, I want to give you five questions to think about when making a decision that will impact your schedule and your time.

1. *Can I do it?*

   This is the first and most obvious question to consider. If you aren't available, then it's an easy no. If you are available, you can move on to the next four questions.

2. *Is this a priority for me right now?*

   Even if you are available, you need to consider if this is a priority to you. Look at your priorities for this season like we talked about in the previous chapter. Look at your priorities for the week that this falls in. Is this in line with those priorities? Is it important to you? Do you actually care about doing it? Stephen Covey says, "Don't prioritize your schedule. Schedule your priorities." If this thing is not a priority, it probably shouldn't make the cut and get a spot on your calendar.

3. *What will I not be able to do if I do this?*

   We rarely, if ever, ask this question. We don't consider the opportunity cost of the decisions we make. We just see the request in front of us, the person with the pleading look on their face, or the desperate approach in their text or email, and we decide based on that. But for everything you say yes to, you have to say no to a lot of other things. You need to make sure you are okay with all of those nos before you say yes.

Let's go back to my soccer example. If I said yes to coaching soccer again, what would I *not* be able to do? I wouldn't be able to cancel if Carter or I were sick or our family wanted to go out of town. I wouldn't be able to sleep in on a Saturday and have my husband take him to the game. I wouldn't be able to sit on the sidelines and relax. I wouldn't have as much family time in the evenings because I'd be planning practices and communicating details for games to parents. There are a lot of things I wouldn't be able to do if I said yes to that request.

And the same is true for you. Every time you say yes to something, there are things you aren't able to do because of that decision. Ask yourself what those things are, and it will help you consider if it's worth it to you before you commit.

4. *How will this affect my family?*
    My default answer to requests is yes—anytime, any-where, to anyone. I learned pretty early on in my mar-riage, though, that my husband doesn't operate this

way. So when I would fill up our social calendar with events every single night of the week, he was not only exhausted, he was irritated! Since I wanted to attend all those things, it never occurred to me that he didn't. Now I know to ask him—whether it's about a social event, a night out with friends, or even work travel.

When I tell people that I ask my husband before I commit to something, sometimes they get offended. But they've got the wrong idea about what I mean by that. We are both adults who can make our own decisions, of course. But the reality is, those decisions impact each other. It is out of respect for each other's time that we ask.

When I ask Matt if he's okay with me working out in the morning before work, I am showing him that I understand the consequences of that. If I'm gone, he's "on duty" for the kids by himself. I also ask because I want to make sure he doesn't have a work meeting or something else going on, which he *has* many times before! And if I have a work event or trip coming up, I run that by him too. Work is one of those things I love most, and it's easy to say yes to everything that pops up, but Matt is a great source of insight for me. When I ask him what he thinks, he helps me see if I'm overcommitting myself, which helps me protect my time better.

When you share your plans with your spouse or older kids and get their input, it shows them that you understand that your decisions impact them. You aren't only concerned with protecting your own time, but you are also considerate of the people who are most important to you.

5. *Will I want to do it then?*

You might want to do it right now. I do. I want to do everything right now. It sounds like a fantastic idea, *right now.* Hosting the PTA at my house on a Sunday night? Absolutely! Signing up for a Bible study that meets before work on Mondays? For sure! Agreeing to a speaking event in Nowhere, Kansas, on a Saturday in February? Totally! When I ask myself now if I want to do it, the answer is almost always a yes! That's why I need to slow down and ask myself a different question. I need to ask myself if I will want to do it *then.*

Do I really want to feel rushed every Monday morning to make it to Bible study? Do I really want to spend my weekend cooking and cleaning to host a party on Sunday night? Do I really want to be away from my kids for *another* weekend? Probably not. See how this changes your answer? Framing it this way helps you project out into the future and think about what you are willing to commit to, or not. It helps you make better decisions and avoid saying yes to things you'll regret down the road.

These five questions will help you process the opportunities that you're faced with and make better decisions. I do want to call out one important thing here, though. This is a guide. It's not a perfect formula. There will be times when God puts someone in your path and you just feel compelled to drop everything and help them or bless them and listen to them. In those moments, this guide goes out the window and you should always listen to the Spirit within you. But outside of those divine moments when you feel God prompting you in a way that only he can, these questions can help you put thought and intentionality into how you spend your time so that you can use it on the right things.

When You *Still* Feel Stuck

Even when you ask yourself the five questions above, you still might find yourself at a fork in the road, not knowing which route to take. You'll have internal debates, and each side will make a strong argument about which decision is right. When that happens, and it will sometimes, you can ask yourself three additional questions to dig a little deeper and come to a decision.

1. *Is it worth it to them for what it will take out of me?*

    In my early twenties, I had committed myself to doing something (who knows what), and when it came down to actually doing it, I was stressed out and vented to my mom. My mom listened to my dilemma and then said, "Ask yourself, 'Is it worth it to them for what it will take out of me?'" How brilliant is that? This helped me look at my situation differently and made it easier to decide what was best.

    My friend and former roommate Ashley loves to help others. One night years ago, we were sitting in our living room and she was telling me how stressed out she was. She had decided to bake a pie for a friend at work, just because. She hadn't told them she was going to do this, so she didn't have to follow through with it.

    But like with many of us, what started as an idea in her head (*I could bake a pie for them!*) turned into an obligation *(I have to bake a pie for them!)*. As she complained about having to go buy the ingredients and stay up late to bake, I reminded her that she actually didn't have to bake the pie. "But I want to do something nice for them! I planned to do it!" she said.

At this point I asked her the same powerful question my mom had shared with me: "Is it worth it to them for what it's going to take out of you? You're going to go to the grocery store at 8:00 p.m. and stay up for hours baking this thing from scratch. That's taking a lot out of you. Is this nice gesture they aren't even expecting really worth that? What if you waited until a weekend when you have more time and it isn't going to stress you out?"

Asking this question helps you discern which efforts are worth it and which ones are not. If it's worth it, great! You can do it. And if not, you can let go of the pressure you were feeling. You can then make better decisions with your time and energy and protect your schedule and your sanity.

2. *Which decision will I regret?*

It's amazing how much clarity you can get by looking at your options through the lens of potential regret. Which decision will you regret? Going on that trip or not going? Committing to that responsibility or passing on it? Accepting that calendar invitation or declining?

When you ask yourself which you will regret, it helps you project out into the future and think about the opportunity differently.

Several years ago, Matt and I signed up to run the Memphis marathon. We had been diligent about training for the December race, and by October we completed our eighteen-mile training run. We only had one more twenty-mile practice to go before tapering off before race day. But in the early part of November, Matt's best friends from college decided to go camping for one of the guys' birthdays. It was the same weekend as the race.

When Matt told me about it, I could tell he was bummed to miss out. Who wouldn't be? With wives and babies and mortgages and careers and responsibilities, these guys almost never got together anymore. I typically try to avoid telling Matt what he *should* do, but sometimes I can't resist giving my opinion.

"Well, I really think you should go," I said. "We've run a thousand races and we will run a thousand more, but weekends like this don't happen often. You won't regret going. You *will* regret *not* going." After he thought about it, he agreed and decided to go camping with the guys instead of racing that weekend. They had an awesome time, and it's a memory he will never forget. Sometimes, when your options are overwhelming or your choice isn't clear, simply asking which scenario you'd regret can help you know what to do in the moment.

3. *Which decision makes me feel relieved?*

Similar to the previous question but from the other perspective, this question helps you project out into the future and think about the opportunity differently. When I think in terms of "relief," usually one decision clearly trumps the other.

My friend Sophie actually used this strategy when making a decision about the holidays one year. She was feeling pressure to host Thanksgiving dinner for her whole family. Her sister had asked her to do it, and she felt torn on whether or not to commit. With everyone together, it was going to be more than twenty-five people, and with everything else she had going on, Sophie felt exhausted at the very thought of it. She went back and forth on the pros and cons of each choice, but when she asked herself which option made her feel relieved—hosting her family for Thanksgiving or not—the answer was clear. That wasn't her year to host. When she told her sister her decision, Sophie's shoulders physically relaxed and she breathed a sigh of relief. When your body responds in this way to making a decision, you can almost always guarantee it was the right one.

Each of the above questions are examples of how I make decisions in my life. They help me sort through my options to make the best choice. But you might have some others to add as well. I asked my friends how they make decisions, and they had a variety of responses. My friend Beth asks herself, "Will this glorify God?" and "Do I have the energy for this?" while my friend Sarah asks herself, "What are the logistics if I say yes?" and "Will this require me to shower and wear normal clothes?" *Ha!* I love all of these examples because I can relate to each of them as well.

There isn't a perfect formula for decision-making, and like I said before, there will be times that God asks you to do something that doesn't fit perfectly in your schedule. But the rest of the time, you can use these questions and any of your own to help you make the best decision for you.

THIS IS WHO YOU ARE

Oprah Winfrey once said, "How you spend your time defines who you are." If you feel bad about how you spend your time, you will feel bad about who you are. And if you feel bad about who you are, you'll feel bad about everything else too. You'll say yes when you need to say no. You'll make decisions you regret and beat yourself up for it later. You'll move to the back of the line in your own life and then you'll be angry you're there. You'll be anxious and overwhelmed, conflicted and guilt-ridden. You'll play the martyr, continuing to put everyone else first as an excuse to live your life grumpy, rushed, and overcommitted. And when you do, everyone loses.

> **It's important to set boundaries and protect what matters. It's not selfish; it's self-preservation and it's smart.**

You know that feeling, don't you? I sure do. It's being impatient with your kids, unhappy with your spouse, and easily frustrated at work because you haven't had even two free minutes for yourself to do what actually matters to you. That's why it's so important to make the right decisions about what you say yes to and what you say no to. It's important to set boundaries and protect what matters. It's not selfish; it's self-preservation and it's smart.

Whether you realize it or not, when you do this, everyone in your life benefits. You're a better spouse, parent, leader, friend, and overall human being when you're spending your life on what matters most to you. And the great news is that the person in control of your calendar and your commitments is you. No one else. You already have the power and control that you need to create the life you want to lead. It might just be time to flex your confidence muscle and actually use it.

JOURNAL QUESTIONS FOR REFLECTION

1. What does confidence mean to you?
2. How have you made decisions in the past about how you spend your time?
3. How do you feel about saying no and setting boundaries?

Challenge: Your challenge for chapter 6 is to change how you make decisions by setting boundaries and by asking better questions before you commit to something. Use the worksheet for chapter 6: *Change How You Make Decisions* in your digital workbook at ramseysolutions.com/tbyt to guide you. This worksheet can also help you talk to your spouse about how each of you makes decisions with your time so that you can get on the same page.

CHAPTER 7

STEP 5:
BE PRESENT FOR WHAT MATTERS

When I dropped Carter off at daycare for the very first time when he was four months old, I was a wreck. I tried to hold back the tears as I carried him to his classroom and handed his teacher his tiny backpack full of bottles. Then as soon as I got back in my car, I lost it. Full-on sobbing and ugly-crying. I pulled myself together enough to drive to my office, which was a whole 0.25 miles away, and as I did, tears streamed down my face. I kept looking through the rearview mirror, worrying about Carter. *What if he's sad? What if he gets sick? What if he misses me? Is he okay? What if he needs me? Will they call?* Worries flooded my mind as I drove to work that day.

In that moment, two things that I loved very much—my child and my work—were pulling at me, making me feel conflicted and leading to guilt, stress, and worry. And, honestly, I've felt that way many times since then. Like when I missed speaking somewhere to attend a friend's wedding, or even when I had to choose between two different school events for each of my children. But this is the reality of life. As we've talked about already, our time is finite. We are always going to have to make choices—sometimes hard ones—about where we go and what we do. The problem is that we often focus on the place we aren't instead of focusing on where we are.

You might be rocking it at work during the week but you're worried about your kids while you're there. You might be hanging out with your family on the weekend but worried about all the emails you need to catch up on for work. You might be out to dinner with your friends and feeling guilty for turning down your parents' invitation for a home-cooked meal. Or at your parents' house for dinner and feeling like you're missing out on a night with friends. Whatever it is, you feel guilty. Instead of enjoying where you are, you're thinking about where you aren't. The FOMO that haunts us isn't just about the *fear* of missing out; it's also our problem of *focusing* on missing out.

It's those moments of conflict—when you're doing one thing but feel like you're falling behind on something else— that are robbing you of your peace, joy, and balance. Because, as I mentioned earlier in this book, even if you create the most perfect schedule in the world, if you aren't present for it, you'll miss it. You might be right where you're supposed to be and even want to be, but you're too busy worrying about the places you're not. That's why if we want to shake the guilt and feel any sense of balance, we need to learn to flip our focus. Instead of looking through

> **The fifth step on The Path to Balance is to be present for what matters.**

the rearview mirror, we have to look through the front windshield of our lives so we can experience and appreciate what is in front of us—the very moment we're in. That's why the fifth and final step on The Path to Balance is to be present for what matters. Wherever you are, be there.

BARRIERS TO BEING PRESENT

It sounds nice, doesn't it? *Just be present. It's not that hard. Just be where you are.* If it were that easy, then we wouldn't struggle doing it. But we all know that it's not easy. In our busy lives with so much competing for our attention, not to mention all that we have going on at any given time, it feels almost impossible to focus on what's in front of us. There are a few specific barriers that make this especially difficult though: cell phones, interruptions, and wandering thoughts. These distractions can keep us from focusing on the right thing and being present in the moment we're in.

Cell Phones

Everywhere we go, we see foreheads illuminated by screens. Like we talked about in chapter 4, our addiction to technology is stealing our time, but even more terrifying is that it's stealing our ability to be present. Our culture's obsession with technology is keeping us from having any sense of balance in our lives. And, all too often, nonstop screen time steals our attention away from the important moments happening right in front of us.

We are so used to our phone being in our hands that we feel naked, vulnerable, and uncomfortable without it. Isn't that crazy? If you've ever left your phone at home or lost it for any significant amount of time, you know the feeling of panic of having to go without it. We've become so dependent on and addicted to that one little device that we forget how we ever survived without it (for those of us who are old enough to remember life before cell phones).

Since the entire world is competing for your attention through your phone—whether that's through email or social media or notifications from your different apps—it's nearly impossible to be present in the moment you're in. In *Get Your Life Back*, John Eldredge wrote,

> We talk about unplugging, but we're enchanted—by the endless social media circus of love and hatred, the vapid, alarming, sensational, and unforgivable. We're snagged by every new notification. And while we've always had our individual struggles and heartbreaks to deal with, now we have the tragedies of the entire world delivered to us hourly on our mobile devices.
>
> This is all very hard on the soul. Traumatizing, in fact.[24]

Like a drug, we are addicted to it and damaged by it. It's stealing our joy, presence, and balance; it's stealing our very lives.

There's no such thing as undivided attention anymore. In fact, research shows that people often use two devices at once—watching a show on Netflix while scrolling Instagram, for example.[25] I've done that. Have you? We've become so accustomed to this division of our attention that we don't question it, much less guard against it. The problem with this, of course, is that our attention can't be divided. You can give attention—true thought, focus, and presence—to only one thing at a time. Sure, you can do mindless tasks while working on something that requires attention, such as throwing laundry in the washer while talking on the phone. But you can't actually give your attention to two places at once. Have you ever tried to have a conversation with someone while they're texting? Right. They aren't listening. They can't! Anytime that I have my phone in my hand while watching a movie with my husband, inevitably I have to ask him, "Wait, what just happened?"

It doesn't really matter if you know what happened during every scene of a movie, but what if while scrolling Instagram, you miss your child walking for the first time? What if your teenager is trying to tell you about their day at school and you appear too busy to listen? What if your spouse tells you about an important project at work and you're checked out? What if a good friend is trying to tell you about a struggle they are going through and your fingers are flying through a text to someone else? Our addiction to our phones is damaging our relationships and our ability to be present. Like I said in chapter 1, we're going to know everything about everyone else's lives but completely miss our own. And that's exactly what's happening.

I'll be honest, I struggle with this daily. I'm guessing most of us do. A few years ago, when I realized I needed to stop checking my phone so often, I decided to start asking myself a question every time I was tempted to pick it up: *Is it more important that I know what the outside world is doing right now, or is it more important that I experience what I am doing right now?* This question almost always answers itself. This helps me to not only put things into perspective but also to put down my phone and be truly present with family, friends, or coworkers. It works whether you're mindlessly scrolling Twitter while waiting at a restaurant with your spouse or you're perusing Facebook in the grocery store line while your child is trying to get your attention. Even if you're just enduring something mundane, when you are with someone, they matter more.

In her book, *Calm, Cool, and Connected*, Arlene Pellicane teaches a five-step plan for creating boundaries around technology. The second habit she talks about is to "always put people first." To do this, she uses "the pivot." Here's how it works. When you have technology in your hand and someone walks into the room, that human being takes priority. Your head should physically lift from your phone to acknowledge the person coming, and you should give them your full attention and make eye contact. This sends the message that they are more important than what you're looking at on your phone—which they are.[26]

Another strategy is the phone check. A friend of mine uses a "tech basket" when going out to dinner with friends. She literally brings a basket with her to the restaurant and places it in the center of the table. Everyone has to put their phone face down in the basket at the start of dinner and leave it there the entire time. If anyone reaches for their phone before the bill comes, they have to pay the entire tab! Let's just say, it's an incredibly effective practice that keeps everyone present and engaged. And my guess is these dinners are much more memorable, not to mention more fun.

That seems doable for a quick dinner, but what if you have a family and you're at home all evening? We're all guilty of mindlessly scrolling social media, checking the news or the weather, or sending a quick email or text. And our families pay the price. If you have kids and think they don't notice when you're distracted by your phone, you're wrong. My friend Jeremy told me about something his son said to him one night several years ago while getting tucked into bed. He said, "Daddy, your stories are so much better when you don't have an iPhone in your hand." *Ouch*. Moments like this feel like a punch in the gut. And they should. That's what we need to start making real changes, set real boundaries, and create new habits that move our phones from the pinnacle of our priorities.

> I don't want to miss my life because I am watching someone else live theirs.

In our home, that looks like a phone box on the kitchen counter. When I get home from work each day, my phone goes in the box and it doesn't come out until my kids go to bed. If I was carrying my phone around with me all evening, I would check it repeatedly, and the scary part is, I wouldn't even realize I was doing it! All the while, I'd be missing out on what really mattered and I wouldn't be present with my family.

I love how Rachel Macy Stafford, author of *Hands Free Mama*, talks about this with "The Hands Free Pledge." It says:

> I'm becoming Hands Free. I want to make memories, not to-do lists. I want to feel the squeeze of my child's arms, not the pressure of overcommitment. I want to get lost in conversation with the people I love, not consumed by a sea of unimportant emails. I want to be overwhelmed by sunsets that give me hope, not by overloaded agendas that steal my joy. I want the noise of my life to be a mixture of laughter and gratitude, not the intrusive buzz of cell phones and text messages. I'm letting go of distraction, disconnection, and perfection to live a life that simply, so very simply, consists of what really matters. I'm becoming Hands Free.[27]

I love that. I don't want my children's memories of me to be of my forehead illuminated by a screen. I don't want my spouse, my friends, or my family to think that my phone is more important than they are. I don't want to miss my life because I am watching someone else live theirs. I don't want to be so focused on documenting moments and posting pictures that I don't even get to experience them myself. I want to put my phone down and look up. I want to experience my own life and be present for what matters. And I bet you do too. That's why we have to set boundaries and create habits to help us focus on what's happening right in front of us.

Interruptions

During the 2020 pandemic and quarantine, millions of Americans were forced to work from home. Families were turning playrooms into classrooms and dining rooms into offices. Everyone was doing the best they could with what they had. If you were one of those people juggling work and kids like never before, you know that there were a lot of interruptions. There was little separation between work life and family life, and the whole thing was crazy and comical at times.

On one particular day, I was on a Facebook Live for Business Boutique Academy, my coaching group for women with businesses. I had my computer and light set up and everything was going great. I was in coaching mode, talking fast, waving my hands, and answering the questions that popped up in the chat. In the middle of answering a question, I (and everyone watching the live video) heard a little voice in the background say, "Mommy! I pee-peed in the potty!" It was my son Conley. Of course, I laughed and congratulated Conley on his exciting news. Then he proceeded to walk around the house, very loudly telling every person individually. "Carter, I pee-peed in the potty! Daddy, I pee-peed in the potty!"

The interruption from Conley was hilarious and cute, and I will actually treasure that video clip forever. But interruptions aren't always funny and cute like that one. Sometimes they can be annoying and frustrating, and they can keep us from being able to be present in the moment we're in. It's hard to come across as professional on your Zoom call when your neighbor is mowing their lawn right outside your window, and it's hard to put together a presentation when you have people walking up to your desk every two minutes. Whether you're trying to work on your business or just have a nice conversation with a friend, reducing interruptions when you can will help you be more present, get more done, and have more balance.

One of the ways you can do that is by physically separating your work and your home life as much as possible. Even if you work from home, as many business owners do, I encourage you to have a physical space for your work within your home. When you go into this space—whether it's a craft room, garage, home office, or someplace else—it's a cue for your brain to go into work mode. It's also a visible reminder for your spouse and kids that when you're in there, you're working. It also gives you permission to be "off work" when you leave that space.

And this goes both ways. You're going to have to work hard to reduce interruptions from work cutting into your family time. You can do this by setting boundaries like we talked about in the previous chapter. For example, you may want to place your phone and computer in another room to avoid phone calls, emails, and texts from work.

Unless you are a doctor who is literally on-call, you probably don't have to be as available as you might feel pressured to be. Technology has so many benefits in our world today, but it also has created a culture where we are expected to be "on" and always available. If we get texts and emails all hours of the day and night regarding work, it sends a message that because *someone else* is working around the clock, *we* have to as well. But we don't. It's okay to set boundaries around your personal or family time.

And if you are single or don't have kids, this does not exclude you. You need time to disconnect from work and responsibilities just as much as someone who is juggling a family. In one of my previous jobs, I was assigned the "Manager on Duty" shift on Friday nights every single week for an entire quarter. No matter how many times I asked to be rotated to a different time, my request was ignored, and I had no idea why.

One day, when the next quarter's shifts were posted, I saw that I was on Friday nights again. I walked up to my manager and in a very respectful way asked why: "I don't understand why everyone else seems to get their requests but my request to be moved off of Friday nights for a season isn't. Can you help me understand?"

My manager, who was actually a very nice and well-meaning man, looked me straight in the eye and said, "Well, Christy, everyone else has families, so they want to spend Friday nights with their families. You're single and don't have a family, so it makes the most sense for you to do it." My mouth dropped open in complete shock. I know. The audacity. I responded in a confused tone, though I was absolutely fuming inside. I said, "But just because I'm not married doesn't mean my time doesn't have value to me." I was moved off the shift the next week.

> Even nice, well-intentioned people can ignorantly underestimate someone else's need for balance if their life looks different than their own.

The truth is, even nice, well-intentioned people can ignorantly underestimate someone else's need for balance if their life looks different than their own. Whether you are married or not, have kids or not, are young or not, don't be afraid to speak up for yourself and your needs. You are not responsible for working more or taking on something just because you're the single one, the retired one, the one with no kids, or whatever. Your life is just that: yours. You get to decide how you spend it, and sometimes you have to be willing to speak up and be your own best advocate in order to protect your time.

My friend Jake was telling me a story recently of a typical Saturday morning at his house. Their family starts with a big breakfast together at the kitchen table. The problem is, they live in a neighborhood full of kids who are constantly ringing each other's doorbells to ask friends to play outside. And every Saturday morning, as if on cue, the doorbell would start ringing right as they sat down to eat. Jake would go to the door and let the kids know that his boys could play after breakfast. But that didn't stop another kid from ringing the doorbell ten minutes later. And another. And another. It was nonstop.

Finally, after weeks of this, his wife made a sign with a piece of paper and marker that said, "Please do not ring the doorbell or knock. The boys will come outside when they're able to play. Thank you." Then she taped it next to the doorbell. That immediately put an end to the ringing doorbell so the family could enjoy their breakfast and not be interrupted constantly.

You might have a hundred interruptions a day, whether you're working or not. But that doesn't mean you don't have any control over those interruptions. Sure, some things you have to handle right away. But, more than likely, the interruptions that we feel we must give our attention to in a given moment don't really need our attention right then and there.

As Stephen Covey said, "Most of us spend time on what's urgent and not enough time on what's important." And whether we realize it or not, *urgent* and *important* are not the same thing. When you create boundaries around your work and family time, you reduce interruptions and give yourself the gift of being able to be present for what is important right in front of you.

Wandering Thoughts

How many times have you been driving your car when suddenly you look around and realize you don't remember the last five minutes you were driving? Or worse, you've pulled into your driveway and don't remember much of your drive at all! It's startling, isn't it? And this doesn't just happen when we're driving. We do this while we're reading, while we're listening to a podcast, while we're in church. At some point we snap back into the present moment and think, *Well, shoot. I can't even remember at what point my mind started wandering off.*

This happened to me a couple of months ago. I grabbed a cookie after dinner, and because I got distracted with something else while I was eating it, I didn't even remember eating it! I got the calories but didn't get the enjoyment of it! And this happens to us all the time, doesn't it? A Harvard study found that people aren't really paying attention to what's right in front of them 47 percent of the time![28] *Forty-seven percent!*

Our minds wander so quickly and easily from what's right in front of us that just when we get one thought under control, we get distracted by another, then another. And we're missing out on being truly present in the moment because our minds are running in a hundred different distracted directions. That's why we have to learn to control our thoughts and focus them on where we are right now—on the present.

In her book *Get Out of Your Head,* Jenni Allen says that humans have, on average, 30,000 thoughts a day, and up to 70 percent of those are negative. She wrote, "Learning to capture our thoughts matters. Because how we think shapes how we live."[29] You and I have experienced the results of that whether we realize it or not. On any given day at any given time, your brain is in overdrive. Your mind is bouncing around like a pinball: *Did I ever text Mom back about this weekend? . . . I think we are out of milk . . .*

I need to remember to stop and get some on the way home . . . Oh no, I still haven't bought a present and that party is on . . . Do I know her? She just looked at me like I know her . . . I wonder if he took what I said the wrong way. Wait! What exactly did I say?

And on and on and on all day long. It's hard to be present and enjoy the moment you're in when your mind is bouncing around to twenty-seven other places simultaneously. Another Harvard study determined that "mind-wandering is an excellent predictor of people's happiness. In fact, how often our minds leave the present is a better predictor of our happiness than the activities in which we're engaged."[30] That's fascinating! It doesn't matter as much *what* you're doing. What matters is that you focus on what you're doing—*that* is what actually leads to more happiness.

> It's hard to be present and enjoy the moment you're in when your mind is bouncing around to twenty-seven other places simultaneously.

The great news is that we are actually more in control of our minds than we realize. We don't have to be victims to the onslaught of endless thoughts. We can catch, correct, and redirect our thoughts anytime we realize they're wandering off without our permission. We can consciously control them and force ourselves to focus on what is right in front of us.

Psychologists call this practice "mindfulness." This is a popular term in the yoga and self-help space, and yes, the concept is rooted in Eastern religions. But before you start tagging me on social media, telling me about all your feelings on the concept, I want you to consider how this simple act can help you feel more balanced. Mindfulness is simply the ability to be fully present in the moment. Don't we all want that? I know I do.

One simple way that I try to practice mindfulness is to ask myself a very obvious question: "What is right in front of me?" By reminding myself of what's right in front of me, I bring it back into focus, front and center, and redirect my thoughts to it. The answer to my simple question is always what I should be focusing on. What's right in front of me? Whether it's my daughter grabbing my leg, my coworker talking in a meeting, a neighbor waving as we pass on the street, or just a beautiful sunset right outside my window, when I redirect my thoughts to what's right in front of me—when I practice mindfulness—I allow myself to experience and actually enjoy the moment I'm in. I allow myself to actually enjoy my life.

You don't have to feel like your brain is running off the rails all the time. You have the power to control your thoughts and direct them (and redirect them as needed) to what's right in front of you. But being present won't happen accidentally. With 30,000 thoughts a day, it's going to take effort and intentionality to retrain your brain to be where your feet are. But with a little practice, you can do it.

THE GIFT EVERYONE WANTS

Leading girls at Young Life camps has been a huge highlight for me over the years. And at every camp, there is a tradition we always keep. Near the end of the week, all the students, leaders, and volunteers cram into the big clubroom and watch the video highlight reel of the girls' life-changing and memorable week. The video team does an amazing job capturing the games and songs, the activities and adventures, and the meals and special moments from the week, and we all sit on the floor to watch it unfold on the big screen. We laugh, cry, and reflect on what an amazing time we all had.

One year, as I sat with my Young Life girls on the floor of the big room, I stopped watching the video and began looking around the room. All 500 high school students sat on the floor with their eyes glued to the big screens. In that moment, I realized something—every single person in this room is thinking the same thing right at this exact moment: *I hope I see myself.*

In a time when teenagers are more addicted to their phones than ever before, not a single person took their eyes off of the video for even a moment. They didn't want to miss the moment that they might appear on the screen, they might be featured, *they might be noticed.*

And the same is true for every single person in our lives. Young or old, male or female, introvert or extrovert—every single person has a deep desire to simply be seen, to be noticed. They want your eye contact and your attention, your love and affection. *They want to be noticed.* When you put your phone down, you're giving people something incredibly rare in the world we live in: your undivided attention. So stop and slow down, put the device away, look your loved ones in the eyes, and spend quality (translation: unrushed and undivided) time with them. When you do, you'll realize that the gift you're giving isn't just for the person you're with. It's also for you, as you get to show up and actually experience your own life.

Flip Your Focus

My friend Tony used to say, "I'm always driving to somewhere that I love. When I'm driving to work, I'm driving to somewhere that I love. And when I'm driving home, I'm driving to somewhere that I love." What I love about Tony's perspective is how he is always focused on where he's going, not what he's leaving behind. He's already preparing himself to be present wherever he is headed. He isn't thinking about what he just left and worrying about what hasn't been done. He is excited about what's in front of him. When you flip your focus to actually experience and enjoy the moment you're in, you start to appreciate your life in a new way.

You realize that one of the reasons you've been feeling out of balance isn't just because you were doing too many things but because you were missing your life altogether, and you don't have to anymore. You don't have to create a perfect 50/50 split between your "work" and your "life" because balance is less about a 50/50 split and more about being 100 percent present wherever you are.

> Balance is less about a 50/50 split and more about being 100 percent present wherever you are.

Now you notice sunsets you never noticed before. You notice the way a friend opens up to you because you took the time to listen, truly listen. You notice how your child's eyes light up when you get down on the floor to play with them. You notice how your breathing deepens and your shoulders relax. You notice how your thoughts no longer bounce around uncontrollably. You begin to focus on what you are doing right now instead of what you aren't doing. You're proud of what you've accomplished instead of feeling guilty for what you've left undone. You feel less stressed because you no longer feel like you're falling short. Your life is no longer just full; it's actually fulfilling. You can finally feel free to not only create the life you want but to have the power to be present for it.

Congratulations! You've walked through the five steps in The Path to Balance.

- You've decided what matters most to you.
- You've stopped doing what doesn't matter.
- You've created a schedule that reflects what does matter.
- You've learned to protect what matters.
- You understand how to be present for what matters.

But this path isn't something you start and finish and never revisit again. It's a cycle, with ebbs and flows, just like life. You will walk through situations that will take all the work you've done to create balance and completely upend it. You may enter a new life stage with your work, family, or priorities. Or you might enter a new season as God gently leads you in a new direction or toward a new dream.

That's why you'll want to revisit The Path to Balance as the seasons of your life change. When you reset and start at Step 1, decide what matters to you in that new season, and complete all the steps that follow, you can create a new version of balance—a version that better suits you in your new season of life. And we are going to talk about how to do just that in the final chapter!

JOURNAL QUESTIONS FOR REFLECTION

1. What stood out to you from this chapter as we talked about how being present affects every aspect of our lives, even our sense of balance?
2. Can you think of a few times when you were missing the moment because you were thinking about everything you *weren't* doing?
3. What is the biggest barrier that keeps you from being present?

Challenge: Your challenge for chapter 7 is to create habits to help you stay present. Use the worksheet for chapter 7: *Create Habits to Help You Stay Present* in your digital workbook at ramseysolutions.com/tbyt to guide you. Write out new habits you want to create that will help you resist (or manage) the barriers to balance we covered in this chapter, as well as any others you might want to add. Like each of the topics we've covered in this book, this is another great opportunity to connect with your spouse and get on the same page about what each of you values and wants for your lives.

CHAPTER 8

CREATING BALANCE IN EVERY SEASON

Cody couldn't believe it; he had been laid off. His family's health insurance depended on his employee benefits, and to make matters worse, he and his wife had a baby on the way. He was anxious and overwhelmed. He was panicked about the present and fearful about the future. He didn't know how he was going to pay his bills or find a new job. And the daily news headlines about unemployment only reminded him of how bad this whole thing was. He wanted to take care of his family, but he had no idea how he was supposed to do that now. He felt like a failure. No, he *was* a failure. Or that's how it seemed anyway.

When you go through something really hard or painful like Cody, it's easy to feel the same way. You might look at your situation and draw conclusions about who you are. You were laid off from your job, so you feel like a failure. You put your business on hold for a season, so you feel like a quitter. You don't work outside the home, so you feel you're "just" a mom. You didn't reach a certain goal, so you feel you're a disappointment. Whatever the situation may be, a gavel of judgment comes down on your identity, and the verdict isn't good.

We all do that, don't we? We look at our situation and draw conclusions about who we are. But this thinking isn't healthy *or* accurate. The season of your life doesn't define you. Your season is simply *where* you are, not *who* you are. Seasons can change, and they will. Each season will affect different areas of your life, from your priorities to your schedule and even your energy level. That's why you will want to use The Path to Balance as a guide to help you define and create balance in every new season. If you're going to do that, you need to acknowledge the season you are in so that you can adapt to it as you go.

ACKNOWLEDGE THE SEASON YOU ARE IN

Soon after having Carter, I went to lunch with my friend Eve. "How's it going?" she asked. "It's hard!" I answered honestly. One of the things I love about Eve is how matter-of-fact she is. Without missing a beat, she asked, "Well, you know why it's so hard, don't you?" I wanted to answer: *Because this tiny human never, ever, ever sleeps and won't nurse and I don't know what he wants and I'll never feel normal again?* But I didn't. Instead, I just waited for Eve to tell me the answer to her own question: "Because you're still trying to do everything you did before kids," she said. "But now you have a baby. And you can't do everything you did before kids. That *is* hard."

And just like that, Eve cut through my drama and summarized my situation. Yes, babies are hard and you don't get a lot of sleep. But she was right. I didn't realize how different (and difficult) that new season of life would be. I naively expected that I could do everything I did before my son was born. No matter how many times I tried to do everything, I kept falling short. I needed to acknowledge that I was in a new season of life. And this is what we all need to do when important parts of our lives shift and change.

Since life balance is about doing the right things at the *right time*, it's only logical that those right things will change as our lives change. What balance looks like to me as a mom of three young kids is very different from what it looked like as a single woman in my twenties, and it will be different when my kids are teenagers. My version of balance looks different at work during a year when I am launching a new book compared to when I am in a slower season. What balance looks like in my life can even change between calendar seasons, like from summer to fall. The same will be true for you.

You may be in a season of searching for a new job or starting a small business, or you might be in a season of staying home with your small children. Your schedule could look completely different because you now have all your kids in school—or off to college and careers. You may be recently married, or you may be recently divorced. You might be going through a really easy, fun, and exciting season of life, or you might be going through one that is heartbreaking and just plain hard.

No matter your season, there's an ebb and flow to our lives, and these ebbs and flows affect how we feel, what is important to us, and in a practical way, what goes on our schedules. By acknowledging the season we are in, we can then work to align our lives with the right things at the right time. That's why, as you follow The Path to Balance, you need to acknowledge the season you're in. Then once you acknowledge it, you can begin to adapt to it.

ADAPT TO THE SEASON YOU ARE IN

As your life changes, you'll need to give yourself permission to rethink your version of balance so that you can adapt to the new season you are in. What matters most to you at any given time will often be determined by the season you're in. New things will most likely move to a higher level of importance on your priorities list, and old things will either drop down or completely fall off. I know we don't like trade-offs, but as long as we keep trying to add things to our already-full plates even when things change, we are going to keep feeling out of balance. We've got to stop holding our feet to the fire for old plans and expectations after everything has changed. Because when our season changes, our lives need to reflect that.

For example, when you're in a season with little kids, your parenting responsibilities are very physical and hands-on. You're probably burning 6,000 calories a day just running around after your children, keeping them alive, breaking up fights with their siblings, getting them milk and snacks and lunch and then more snacks, and then there's bath time and teeth brushing and bedtime. By the end of the day, all you want to do is collapse on the couch or in bed. This season is physically exhausting. You can adapt to this season by cutting back on outside commitments, shooting for an earlier bedtime for yourself, and giving yourself grace on keeping the house clean, for example. You can adjust your expectations of yourself and others to adapt to the season you're in.

If you are an empty nester, the season you are in may look completely different. You may have more time, energy, and opportunities to try new things. You can adapt to this season by exploring things you didn't have time to do when your kids were at home. Maybe you take a class, volunteer, start a business, or travel the country with your spouse in an RV. Maybe you do something completely different as you embrace this season and adapt to it.

My friend Michelle is an educator in the Nashville area. She wanted to give her all to her career educating kids and supporting teachers in schools, and as a single woman she was able to. But all of that changed in 2011 when she found out about three children who needed a safe home to go to, and she felt God strongly leading her to provide that for them. Overnight, she became a foster mom to two little girls, a four-year-old and a nine-month-old, and their two-year-old brother who was in the hospital fighting for his life.

Michelle went from having her evenings and weekends to do what she wanted, to feeding, changing diapers, doing day-care drop-offs, and tucking children into bed at night. There was no easing into parenting for Michelle. Her life literally changed in an instant one Sunday morning when two little girls were dropped off at her home. She was immediately the primary caretaker to them, and a month later to their brother, who was released from the hospital and needed ongoing therapy.

Fast-forward nearly three years, and Michelle legally became "Mom" to all three children. She says she never would have imagined her story being written this way, but it is truly her biggest dream come true. Michelle's story is inspiring, and it also shows that the seasons of our lives can change dramatically—sometimes overnight. Michelle was able to adjust her priorities and schedule to adapt to the season she was in, which was completely different than what she expected or even had planned.

When you acknowledge the season you're in and are willing to adapt to it, you're able to unapologetically make decisions that are best for you right now. You will also experience each season differently because of it. Where you used to beat yourself up for falling short, you will find grace. Where you used to be discouraged when expectations weren't met, you will find peace. Where you used to feel hopeless, you will find hope. That's why, wherever you are right now when you're reading this, give yourself permission to acknowledge the season you're in and adapt to it. This will not only help you enjoy it and make the most of it, but it will also help you feel balanced.

DON'T WISH IT AWAY

When we are in the thick of it, whatever *it* is at the time, it's so easy to focus on what's wrong and hard about our situation. Before our dog Jackson passed away, I used to get so frustrated that he would track mud all over the carpet every time it rained outside. Or I would complain about how his black fur gathered in clumps around our house. While those things were frustrating, they were also simply downsides to having a dog. But you know what? There were so many amazing things about having Jackson. He would get so excited every time you came home, even if you'd only been gone five minutes. His tail would wag and he would seem to smile when you played with him in the backyard. Now that Jackson's gone, I'd give anything to have those mud tracks on the carpet and clumps of fur around the house. Those small annoyances of having a dog aren't what I remember most. I remember the good things.

We often focus on the good in our past and the pain in our present, don't we? Unfortunately, this means we often only appreciate something when it's gone. But if we live our lives this way, we don't get to enjoy anything while we're actually experiencing it. We spend our whole lives wishing the moment away, longing for the past or dreaming for the future.

We look back on our childhood and teen years with longing because we were free of responsibility, but we desperately wanted more freedom and independence at the time. We look back on our first tiny apartment fondly, but when we lived there, we couldn't wait to have more space. We look back on college years nostalgically, but when we were in college, we couldn't wait to get out on our own and make our own money. This hits you hard every time an older woman watches you trying to wrangle your kids at the grocery store and then smiles and says, "Enjoy this, because it goes by too fast!" We think, *Does it?! Because we haven't had more than six hours of sleep at night in who knows when or a warm meal since they were born!* But honestly, she's right.

Country artist Trace Adkins has a song called "You're Gonna Miss This," and it brings tears to my eyes every time I hear it. It's about a girl who is always focused on the next thing. When she's in an apartment, she wants a big house filled with babies. When she has babies, she apologizes for everyone screaming. And each time the chorus plays, someone older than her is reminding her that one day she's going to miss this. I don't know about you, but I can relate to that girl. If I'm not careful, I can be so focused on moving to the *next* season that I miss what's happening right *now*. I think a lot of people feel that way.

Last year, as I was conducting phone interviews for research, I noticed something in every conversation. Regardless of the person's age, marital status, profession, number of kids (or if they had kids at all), every person said these five words: "But when things slow down . . ."

"But when things slow down . . . I'll start that ministry."

"But when things slow down . . . I'll take a vacation."

"But when things slow down . . . I'll . . ."

They keep waiting for the next season of life to get easier and better. They keep waiting to be able to enjoy their life. But it never happens because, regardless of what season they are in, they want the next one. The finish line always moves. And season after season, year after year, they live their entire lives waiting for what is next but completely missing what is right in front of them. I don't want to be like that, and I bet you don't either.

THE SIMPLE TRICK TO ENJOYING EVERY SEASON

I remember hearing a tale years ago about a farmer and two travelers. The first traveler was walking down the road and stopped to ask the farmer working in the field, "What sort of people live in the next town?" The farmer responded with a question, "What were the people like where you've come from?" The traveler answered, "They were terrible. Troublemakers and lazy and selfish. Not one of them could be trusted." The farmer replied, "Well, I'm afraid that you'll find the same kind of people in the next town." The traveler was disappointed and went on his way as the farmer returned to his work in the field.

A while later, another traveler came from the same direction and stopped to chat with the farmer. The traveler asked him the same question: "What sort of people live in the next town?" The farmer replied again, "What were the people like where you've come from?" The traveler responded, "They were the best people in the world. Hardworking, honest, and friendly. I'm sad to leave them." "Don't worry," reassured the farmer. "You'll find the same kind of people in the next town."

There is a lesson in this story for all of us. Wherever you are in life, you'll find what you're looking for. In any season, if you're looking for reasons to be sad, disappointed, and angry, you'll find them. And if you're looking for reasons to be happy, grateful, and excited, you'll find those too.

If you've ever been on a mission trip, you know this all too well. In 2011, I had an opportunity to visit the Dominican Republic with my church, and I was blown away by how joyful the people were. They had almost nothing. They lived in mud huts. Their clothes were dirty and torn and they barely had enough food to eat. Yet they were the most grateful, loving, and joyful people I've ever met. When I remember them, I always feel convicted at my lack of gratitude, especially when I have so much to be thankful for. Regardless of how much you have or don't have, you can always find things to be grateful for. Oprah Winfrey says, "What you focus on expands. When you focus on the goodness in life, you create more of it." The key to enjoying anything in life is to look for things to be grateful for. When you do, you'll find what you're looking for.

This takes practice. And the more you practice focusing on the good, the more this becomes a habit for you. I've tried to be more intentional about this in recent years. When I dread going to the grocery store, I stop and thank God that I have money to buy groceries. When I am frustrated that I have to park far away, I thank God for my legs and the fact that I can walk. When my kids leave their bikes in the driveway and I can't even park my own car, I thank God I have healthy and active children. I love the quote, "The best way to have what you want is to want what you have." The more I practice being grateful for what I have, the more I appreciate every amazing thing about my life in every season.

> **The key to enjoying anything in life is to look for things to be grateful for. When you do, you'll find what you're looking for.**

When you focus on the good in the season you're in, it helps you to not only resist the temptation to wish it away, but it also helps you really soak in what matters most. My best friend, Jenny, who was a big-time career woman for years and then decided to stay home with her kids, said to me once, "I love being able to be home with my children, which I know isn't for everyone. I sometimes feel like I'm getting behind on the career front, though. But then I try to shift my focus and ask myself, "What if I could get a glimpse of my future and see myself doing something I'm passionate about? How much more could I enjoy this season I am in?" When you change your attitude and appreciate the good in this moment right here and now, it helps you enjoy the season you're in, be more present, and feel more balanced.

WHAT IF MY SEASON SUCKS?

Like Cody who was laid off, some seasons just suck. They just do. Maybe your extended family can't get along or your kids are causing new levels of chaos. Maybe you feel like you just can't get ahead or get it together. Or your business or marriage is hanging on by a thread. Perhaps you lost a job or a dream or a loved one. The season you're in might be heartbreaking and gut-wrenching, or it might just be irritating. Whatever it is, you're having a hard time, and you feel the furthest you've ever been from balanced. I hear you, and I know because I've been in some of those places before too.

I don't know about you, but I tend to treat those seasons like I am in one of those escape games where my only objective in the world is to *get out*. Rather than finding joy and gratitude in the moment, I'm looking desperately for an emergency exit.

The idea of finding balance in that situation seems laughable. I just want to survive whatever it is and get out as fast as possible.

I usually refer to these seasons in my life as the "wilderness" because that's what they feel like. They feel scary and lonely and really hard. Like those escape games, I just wanted to find the exit—fast. The good news is that there *is* an exit. If you're in a really hard season, it will not be this hard forever. It won't. The bad news is that it may not come as quickly as you'd like. This season you're in is just that—a season. It might be a few weeks or a few months or a few years, but it will not be forever. Whatever season you find yourself in, there are a few things that can help you survive it. Those are: prayer, purpose, and a plan.

> This season you're in is just that—a season. It might be a few weeks or a few months or a few years, but it will not be forever.

Prayer

Kristi McLelland is a brilliant Bible teacher and a new friend of mine. While I think of her as a Bible teacher, she would actually call herself a "biblical culturalist," which just means she brings the original context of the Bible to our world. She helps us understand how it was originally written and intended. One of the things that Kristi has taught me is how differently the seasons of wilderness were viewed during Jesus's time on earth.

According to biblical translation, the Hebrew word for *wilderness* is *midbar*. The Hebrew word for *word* is *davar*. There is a saying in the Middle East among Jewish people: "davar in the midbar," which means "word in the wilderness."

Jewish people didn't view the wilderness as something to escape from, like I often do. Rather, they saw it as an opportunity to meet with God and hear from him in a way that could only happen there. They wanted to get their "davar in the midbar" or their "word in the wilderness."

How differently would we view our own wilderness seasons in life if we saw them as opportunities to meet with God and hear from him? And that's exactly what prayer is—an opportunity to meet with God.

Sometimes we look to God more desperately and listen more intently in the wilderness than any other time in our lives. There might just be something he wants to show us, teach us, or tell us. When we're going through a particularly difficult season, we can pray and ask God to give us a word in the wilderness.

You might be looking for an emergency exit right now in this season you're in, but God actually might have you right where he wants you. He wants to do something in you, right now in this wilderness, that can't happen any other way. When you cry out to God and pray, I believe he will give you strength to survive the season you're in and grace to get through it. He might even give you a "davar in the midbar."

Purpose

I know a recent college graduate named Tracy who took the first job she was offered—as an assistant to a VP of a small company. She didn't have much real-world work experience, so she knew she needed to start somewhere. But as the weeks and months went by, she began to question how she was spending her days. Her job wasn't super fulfilling. Her boss and coworkers were really nice, but there was no career path in her current role—at least that she knew of.

The wide-eyed dream Tracy had after graduation to work someplace meaningful and spend her days serving others was diminishing with each day. She thought, *Is this what being an adult looks like? You work a job you aren't really passionate about just to pay your bills? Surely there is more to life than this.*

So many people have experienced a season where they feel lost and purposeless like Tracy. Maybe you have too. While talking with Elisabeth Hasselbeck on *The Christy Wright Show* a while back, something she said stuck with me: "If God has purpose in your placement, then it is our calling to inject passion into our placement. Decide to have passion for what you're doing." That may be hard, but it's also great advice. Does that mean you have to love the job you're in or resign yourself to doing it forever? Of course not.

But you can choose to inject your own sense of passion into what you're doing, no matter what it is. So how do we do that? We choose it. We don't have to wait to *feel* passionate to choose to *be* passionate. We don't have to wait to know God's purpose to choose to show up with a sense of purpose. We don't have to wait for the perfect job to have a good attitude, to do our best, and to learn and grow. We don't have to wait for circumstances that deserve our enthusiasm to choose to be enthusiastic.

> **Stop waiting around to feel passionate or find your purpose, and instead, inject passion into your placement.**

If God has placed you where you are, you can choose to have passion there. Stop waiting around to feel passionate or find your purpose, and instead, inject passion into your placement. When you do, you're being faithful to where God has you right now, which is a pretty good purpose after all anyway.

A Plan

Years ago, after speaking at a Christian women's event, a woman came up to me to ask a question. She said, "I'm just waiting for God to tell me what to do. I've been waiting for about seven years, but he still hasn't showed me. What do I do?" It was all I could do not to say, "Sister, you gotta get moving! God can turn a moving vehicle, but he can't turn a stalled car!"

If you're in a season of life that you want out of, you have a part to play. The challenges you're facing and the pain you're experiencing might be something God is taking you through to stretch you or grow you, or it might be a sign you need to do something different. If your marriage is hanging on by a thread, it's time to get to a counselor and start working toward a solution. If you've been miserable in your job for five years and you just keep waiting for something to change, it's time for you to start working on a plan to do something different.

Your pain can sometimes be a sign that God is pointing you in a new direction—the direction he wants you to go. In addition to praying and injecting passion into what you're doing, it's also a good time to work on a plan to make your situation better. We need to pray like it all depends on God but work like it all depends on us.

Maybe you're in a season of struggling financially. You're barely getting by, and you don't know why you keep living paycheck to paycheck. You can pray for God to provide for you. You can even have gratitude for what you have and how you're able to get by. But it's also time to work on a plan to make your situation better. It's time to get on a budget and to figure out how to earn more or spend less—or both.

The company I work for, Ramsey Solutions, was built on a passion to help people become debt-free, which is why this hits close to home for me. I remember when I had to dig my way out of debt years ago. It was hard, but I promise you, it changed my life and I've never looked back. You don't have to live your life barely getting by. You can do something today that will change your life forever. Listen to *The Ramsey Show* to get inspired. Read a book like *The Total Money Makeover* to get a plan. Or better yet, download Ramsey+ to get a complete money-management system to help you reach your goals. Whatever you do, do *something*.

Don't sit on the couch for seven years waiting for God to show you what to do. Get up, get moving, and start working on a solution. And then watch how God meets you right where you are and gives you the hope you need to change your life and your legacy.

SEE GOD IN EVERY SEASON

When my mom woke up me at two and three in the morning to take me to her cake shop to bake every day when I was little, I didn't see much purpose in that. When my friend invited me to Young Life as a sophomore in high school, it didn't seem super significant. When I was mucking stalls in a barn and breaking up ice in a trough for horses on a farm in the winter in my early twenties, it was anything but fun. When I joined a running group in my late twenties to train for a marathon, it wasn't a major milestone. At the time, nothing about those seasons or any others seemed significant or life-changing. But as I look back on the different seasons of my life now, I can see God's hand in each of them.

For example, growing up in my mom's business gave me the heart for helping women start businesses. I gave my heart to God on a chilly fall night at SharpTop Cove at Young Life camp that sophomore year. I got to experience starting my first side business boarding horses on the farm, and I met my husband training for that marathon. Those are just a few examples of how God used things that seemed insignificant—or even difficult—at the time for my good. Romans 8:28 says, "We know that all things work together for good to those who love God" (NKJV). And it's true.

I like to think that for each of our lives, God is creating a beautiful quilt, and each quilt square is a season. When you look at a tiny scrap of fabric by itself, it doesn't seem very special, just like many of the seasons we go through. Some seasons are hard and heartbreaking. Some are exhausting and feel like they will last forever. Some are fun and full of laughter. And others don't feel particularly significant at all. But as God pieces them together over time, we can look back in awe of how he has sewn different seasons of our lives together to make something beautiful.

God has given you this one life. Don't waste it on things that don't matter to you or wish it away and miss the moment you're in. You've done the hard work to follow The Path to Balance. You've figured out what matters to you and stopped doing what doesn't matter. You've created a calendar that reflects what matters and learned how to protect it. You know how to be present for what matters.

And, finally, you've learned to acknowledge and adapt to the season you are in so that The Path to Balance can help you in any and every season. When you follow The Path to Balance, you will spend your one life on what actually matters to you. It's in doing so that you finally find the balance you've been looking for. And the best part is, in the process of creating it, you become the person you wanted to be all along.

JOURNAL QUESTIONS FOR REFLECTION

1. How does your perspective change when you realize this is just a season?

2. How can you inject passion into your placement to find purpose in this season?

3. What plan do you want to start working on to improve your situation?

Challenge: Your challenge for chapter 8 is to understand the season you're in. Use the worksheet for chapter 8: *Understand the Season You're In* in your digital workbook at ramseysolutions .com/tbyt to guide you. This worksheet will help you not only understand this season but also adapt to it so you can make the most of it. This is another great opportunity to get on the same page with your spouse about how each of you are feeling and experiencing this season, individually and together.

CONCLUSION

"May the righteous be glad and rejoice before God;
may they be happy and joyful." —Psalm 68:3

I remember August 2010 like it was yesterday. It might seem odd to remember an entire month from so long ago, but there was something so special about it. It was the month that Matt and I started dating. We had been friends for months, but when we started dating, it was as if God opened my eyes to the most amazing man that had been right in front of me.

We hung out the entire month of August, attending concerts, going on dates, and running races. (Yes, that was and still is our idea of a good time!) We had more fun in that one month than I had had in a really long time, and I laughed nonstop. I was so completely and overwhelmingly just . . . *happy*. That is just one example of the *countless* times in my life I have been really happy. I want to be happy in my life, and I'm sure you do too.

We've spent a lot of time talking about what balance is and how to create it. I also think that when we say we want to have balance, what we're really saying is that we just want to be happy—happy with how we spend our time and happy with how we live our lives. Most of all, I believe that we want to be happy *in* our lives. And you know what? When you create the balance we've been talking about, you can be.

IT'S OKAY TO WANT TO BE HAPPY

But somehow this word *happy* has gotten a bad rap—at least in Christian culture. "God doesn't promise that we'll be happy," we hear again and again. Instead, we should "choose joy." Sound familiar? While I do think we should choose joy, "choosing joy" feels different for some reason—like the consolation prize when you can't just be downright happy.

According to author Alli Worthington, the idea that joy is somehow more holy than happiness is a concept that only became popular about a hundred years ago. When she released her book *The Year of Living Happy*, she shared something so interesting with me. She noted, "There's nothing in the Bible that separates the concepts of joy and happiness. They have the same meaning according to the original languages of Scripture. So many of the words our English Bible uses—*delight, joy, gladness*—are actually synonyms for the original Hebrew and Greek words that mean *happiness*. God tells us repeatedly to be happy in Scripture."

I don't know about you, but that's encouraging to me. It feels like the thing I've wanted all along—to just be happy—is an okay thing to want. It's not just okay because I decide it aligns with my own theology, and it's not okay because some self-help guru tells me it's okay. It's okay because the Bible says it's okay. It doesn't mean you or I are selfish for wanting to be happy. After all, God himself tells us to be happy. (And let's be honest, it's pretty hard to show God to the world when you're grumpy!) You can still choose joy, of course. When you get a flat tire in the pouring rain or your child spills the entire gallon of milk trying to make her own cereal, you can choose joy. But the rest of the time, it's okay if you just want to be happy.

What Makes You Happy?

I can tell you what makes me happy. Laughing a lot makes me happy. Also, being outside, exercising, and dancing. Doing things for others makes me happy. I love to play crazy games with my kids, go to concerts, and dress up super fancy with big hair and big earrings and go to a nice restaurant with my husband. Sharing my gifts with the world makes me happy. Girls' nights make me happy. Alone time makes me happy. Supporting ministries I care about, like Young Life, makes me happy. I also love working on things that are creative. All those things make me happy. So you know what I do? I intentionally incorporate those things into my life, which not only makes me feel balanced but makes me happy!

So what makes you happy? What makes you like yourself and your life? What makes you feel like the person God created you to be? Whatever it is, it's okay to want more of that feeling. You don't have to have a big dream or goal you're always hustling for like someone else might, and you don't have to do what anyone else expects you to do. You can do what's right for you, and you can be the person you were created to be. You can create a life that you love and are proud of. You can be happy.

IT'S WHAT YOU DO THAT COUNTS

I don't know who came up with the saying "It's the thought that counts," because, no, it's not. The thought does not count. You're not bragging to your friends about what your spouse *thought* about giving you for your anniversary, and you're not posting on Facebook about what your kids *thought* about earning on their report cards. It's not the thought that counts; it's what you actually *do* that counts.

So even if you've learned exactly what steps to take to create your version of balance and live the life you want, it won't work if you don't do anything about it. Nothing will change unless you change it. But the good news is, you *can* change it.

You can spend your life on "what makes your heart sing," like Katie Davis Majors said, and you can get closer to God and become more sure of yourself, like Annie F. Downs said. You can get comfortable in your own skin, like my friend Eve, and find passion in your placement like Elisabeth Hasselbeck said. You can become the person you want to be in the life you want to lead.

But it starts with you. No one can do it for you. No amount of compliments from others can fill you if you're empty, and no amount of achievements can convince you you're worthy if you don't believe it. No amount of blessings will be enough if you have an ungrateful attitude, and no one can make you happy if you're determined to be unhappy. No one can change your life for you. That's a job that only you can do.

It's your job to decide what matters most to you and to stop doing what doesn't. It's your responsibility to create a calendar that reflects what matters most to you and then to protect it. And it's your job to be present for your life. No one can do it for you. So, friend, actually do it. Do it for your family and friends. Do it for your spouse and your kids. Do it for your impact and your legacy. Do it for you.

Meg Meeker says, "The most powerful way to teach a daughter how to enjoy life is to let her see her mother do the same." Amen to that. Enjoy your life, friend, and watch how the example you set impacts everyone around you.

I want you to create balance, cultivate confidence, and feel peace, but at the end of the day, I really just want you to be happy. This is your one life on this earth, and it's okay for you to want that. My prayer for you is that this path takes you there. I pray that as you follow the steps on The Path to Balance, you take back your time and create a life you love and are proud of. As I said in the first chapter of this book, I pray that you embrace this big, amazing, beautiful life that God created for you to enjoy and that you live it abundantly. I pray that you are happy.

"I have come that they may have life, and that they may have it more abundantly." —John 10:10 NKJV

JOURNAL QUESTIONS FOR REFLECTION

1. How do you feel about "being happy" versus "choosing joy"?
2. Have you ever felt like wanting to be happy is not okay?
3. What does an "abundant life" mean to you?

Challenge: There is one more challenge in your digital workbook at ramseysolutions.com/tbyt to help you identify what makes you happy and check in with yourself as we complete this journey together. You can print new blank copies of this free workbook anytime you need extra pages or want to use the workbook to help you create balance in a new season.

NOTES

1. Larry Ginsberg, "Why Routines Are Important for Mental Health," Hackensack Meridian *Health*, June 2, 2020, https://www.hackensackmeridianhealth.org/HealthU/2020/06/02/why-routines-are-important-for-mental-health/.

2. "How Much Are We Really Attached to Our Phones Physically, Cognitively," dscout, 2016 Study, https://blog.dscout.com/hubfs/downloads/dscout_mobile_touches_study_2016.pdf?_ga=2.12372980.192891102.1602022700-274185888.1602022700.

3. Gary Henderson, "How Much Time Does the Average Person Spend on Social Media?" DigitalMarketing.org, August 24, 2020, https://www.digitalmarketing.org/blog/how-much-time-does-the-average-person-spend-on-social-media.

4. Felix Richter, "The Generation Gap In TV Consumption," Statista, November 20, 2020, https://www.statista.com/chart/15224/daily-tv-consumption-by-us-adults/.

5. Ande Fanning, "No Ordinary Life: Katie Davis' Story of Serving Children in Uganda," Lifeway Young Adults, https://youngadults.lifeway.com/2012/01/no-ordinary-life-katie-davis-story-of-serving-children-in-uganda/.

6. Bill and Pam Farrel, *Men Are Like Waffles—Women Are Like Spaghetti: Understanding and Delighting in Your Differences* (Harvest House Publishers, 2017).

7. "Prioritize," *Oxford English Dictionary*, https://www.lexico.com/en/definition/prioritize.

8. Henry Cloud and John Townsend, *Boundaries: When to Say Yes, How to Say No to Take Control of Your Life* (Zondervan, 1992), 31, emphasis in original.

9. John Mark Comer, *The Ruthless Elimination of Hurry: How to Stay Emotionally Healthy and Spiritually Alive in the Chaos of the Modern World* (Waterbrook, 2019), 37.

10. "Dopamine," *Psychology Today*, https://www.psychologytoday.com/us/basics/dopamine.

11. Comer, *The Ruthless Elimination of Hurry*, 233.

12. "Americans Check Their Phones 96 Times a Day," Asurion, November 21, 2019, https://www.asurion.com/about/press-releases/americans-check-their-phones-96-times-a-day/.

13. Henderson, "How Much Time."

14. Comer, *The Ruthless Elimination of Hurry*, 39.

15. *The Social Dilemma*, directed by Jeff Orlowski (Netflix, 2020).

16. "Here's What Happens When You Don't Get Enough Sleep (And How Much You Really Need a Night)," Cleveland Clinic, June 16, 2020, https://health.clevelandclinic.org/happens-body-dont-get-enough-sleep/.

17. "Do Social Ties Affect Our Health? Exploring the Biology of Relationships," NIH News in Health, February 2017, https://newsinhealth.nih.gov/2017/02/do-social-ties-affect-our-health.

18. Jim Clifton, "The World's Broken Workplace," Gallup, June 13, 2017, https://news.gallup.com/opinion/chairman/212045/world-broken-workplace.aspx?g_source=position1&g_medium=related&g_campaign=tiles.

19. Amy Morin, "7 Science-Backed Reasons You Should Spend More Time Alone," *Forbes*, August 2017, https://www.forbes.com/sites/amymorin/2017/08/05/7-science-backed-reasons-you-should-spend-more-time-alone/?sh=8e11671b7ee3.

20. James Clear, "This 100-Year-Old To-Do List Hack Still Works Like a Charm," *Fast Company*, August 22, 2016, https://www.fastcompany.com/3062946/this-100-year-old-to-do-list-hack-still-works-like-a-charm.

21. Ben Renner, "Survey: Average Person Has Just 4 Hours, 26 Minutes of Free Time Per Week!" Study Finds, April 6, 2019, https://www.studyfinds.org/survey-average-american-free-time-week/.

22. Ilan Shrira, "'Fake It Till You Make It' Turns Out to Be a Good Strategy," *Psychology Today*, January 2, 2016, https://www

.psychologytoday.com/us/blog/the-narcissus-in-all-us/201601/fake-it-till-you-make-it-turns-out-be-good-strategy.

23. Cloud and Townsend, *Boundaries,* 108.

24. John Eldredge, *Get Your Life Back: Everyday Practices for a World Gone Mad* (Nashville: Thomas Nelson, 2020), xii.

25. Sarah Perez, "Nielsen: The Second Screen Is Booming as 45% Often or Always Use Devices While Watching TV," TechCrunch.com, December 12, 2018, https://techcrunch.com/2018/12/12/nielsen-the-second-screen-is-booming-as-45-often-or-always-use-devices-while-watching-tv/.

26. Arlene Pellicane, *Calm, Cool, and Connected: 5 Digital Habits for a More Balanced Life* (Chicago: Moody Publishers, 2017), 55.

27. Rachel Macy Stafford, *Hands Free Mama: A Guide to Putting Down the Phone, Burning the To-Do List, and Letting Go of Perfection to Grasp What Really Matters!* (Zondervan, 2014), page 17.

28. Matthew A. Killingsworth and Daniel T. Gilbert, "A Wandering Mind Is an Unhappy Mind," ScienceMag.org, November 12, 2010, https://wjh-www.harvard.edu/~dtg/KILLINGSWORTH%20&%20GILBERT%20(2010).pdf.

29. Jennie Allen, *Get Out of Your Head: Stopping the Spiral of Toxic Thoughts* (Colorado Springs, CO: WaterBrook, 2020), 5, 10, 50.

30. Scott Mautz, "Harvard Study: 47 Percent of the Time You're Doing This 1 (Fixable) Thing That Kills Your Happiness," Inc.com, May 13, 2019, https://www.inc.com/scott-mautz/harvard-study-47-percent-of-time-youre-doing-this-1-fixable-thing-that-kills-your-happiness.html/.

It's Time to
Get Back to *You*

Is there a part of you that feels lost, or maybe just plain tired? It's time to break free from the demands of life, find grace in this season, and have the confidence to embrace who you were created to be with Christy's devotional.

Reset and rest in the truth of who you are!
ramseysolutions.com/LT

Become the Person You Want to Be

The Christy Wright Show will give you the encouragement you want and the tough-love truth you need to connect with God, take control, and enjoy your life.

Listen or Watch Now